STANDARD METHOD OF MEASUREMENT OF BUILDING WORKS

SEVENTH EDITION REVISED 1998

AMENDMENT 2

age	Rule	Correction
7	A13 Heading	Delete 'work' and insert 'Works'.
3	A32	Delete 'works' and insert 'Works'.
0	A42.1.7	Delete 'materails' and insert 'materials'.
2	C1	Renumber as 'C5'.
5	4	Amend unit column to allow measurement in 'm' and 'nr' as well as 'm² in line with Rules 1–3.
5	Heading	Delete 'C40 continued'.
0	D3	Delete 'Hazardous' and insert 'hazardous'.
3	Heading	"D30 Piling' to be in bolder print (see page 29 for example).
4	D3	Insert horizontal lines above and below the Rule to line up with other horizontal lines. Delete the word 'in'.
5	Heading	Delete 'D30 Piling continued' and insert 'D30 continued' in smaller and bolder print (see page 31 for example). Box in the heading below last (see page 33 for example) and insert on the right half of the page the boxed headings 'Measurement Rules', 'Definition Rules', 'Coverage Rules', and 'Supplementary Information' (see page 36 for example).
	M12	Delete '28–4.1.2.*' and insert '12–16.1.1 and 2.*'
5	26	The 'm²' in the unit column to be deleted and inserted below the line as it refers to Rule 27.
	27.2	Renumber '2' as '1'
7	29.1.2	Delete 'Extention' and insert 'Extension'.
	29.1.3	Delete 'Extention and insert 'Extension'.
	31.1	Delete 'meter' and insert 'metre'.
	33.1.1	Delete '(nr)'.
3	D1	Delete the word 'in'.
	M3(b)	Insert '≤' after 'areas'.
	10.1	Delete 'pocets' and insert 'pockets'.
	E05 Heading	Delete 'constructing' and insert 'construction'.
	Heading	Insert 'in situ' before 'concrete'.
	H40 Heading	Delete 'Glass' and insert 'Glassfibre'.
	D7	Delete 'structured' and insert 'structural'

70	G32 Heading	Delete 'slab' and insert '/rock fibre'.
73	K11 Heading	Amend to read 'Rigid sheet flooring/sheathing/decking/sarking/linings/casings'.
	K14 Heading	Delete 'Glass' and insert Glassfibre'.
	K15 Heading	Delete 'enamelled' and insert 'enamel'.
	K20 Heading	Amend to read 'Timber board flooring/decking/sarking/linings/casings'.
75	H31 Heading	Amend to read 'Metal profiled sheet cladding/covering/siding'.
	H41 Heading	Delete 'Glass' and insert 'Glassfibre'.
80	H70 Heading	Delete 'pre-bonded' and insert 'prebonded'.
	H72 Heading	Delete 'strip sheet' and insert 'strip/sheet'.
	H73 Heading	Delete 'strip sheet' and insert 'strip/sheet'.
	H74 Heading	Delete 'strip sheet' and insert 'strip/sheet'.
	H75 Heading	Delete 'strip sheet' and insert 'strip/sheet'.
83	J20 Heading	Delete 'proof membranes' and insert 'proofing'.
	J30 Heading	Delete 'proof membranes' and insert 'proofing'.
87	K10 Heading	Delete 'lining' and insert 'linings'.
89	Heading	Delete '/K31'.
97	Heading	Insert second heading under first to read 'Q41 Barriers/Guardrails'.
105	Heading	Insert '/M13' after 'M12'.
107	2	Delete 'Beams' and insert 'beams'.
113	M41 Heading	Delete 'in situ' and insert 'In situ'.
120	S8, S9 & S10	Renumber as S7, S8 and S9 respectively.
124	Heading	Delete 'Ironmongery' and insert 'Doors/Window ironmongery'.
131	Q10 Heading	Delete 'accesories' and insert 'accessories'.
137	Q31 Heading	Delete 'Planting' and insert 'External planting'.
	Q32 Heading	Delete 'Indoor planting' and insert 'Internal planting'.
138	11	Renumber as '12' Insert new Rule to read '11 Plant containers' in the first column, '1 Method of fixing' in the second column, '1 Dimensioned description' in the third column and 'nr' in the unit column. Locate below horizontal line between existing Rules 10 and 11 and provide new identical horizontal line below the new Rule.
149	4	Delete 'stair lifts' and insert 'stairlifts'.
156	Heading	Delete 'Y31' and insert 'Y30'.
157	Heading	Delete ' /Y.31'.

Note: This Amendment results from further changes to CAWS headings and/or classifications. The opportunity has been taken to incorporate corrections of minor anomalies, spelling errors etc. As a consequence of the above the Detailed contents on pages 1–7, Appendices A and B on pages 177–182 and the Alphabetical Index on pages 183–190 have been included in the re-printed document.

Standard Method of Measurement of Building Works

smm7

Standard Method of Measurement of Building Works

Authorised by agreement between the Royal Institution of Chartered Surveyors and the Construction Confederation

Seventh Edition Revised 1998

Co-ordinated project information

First Edition, 1922
Second Edition, 1927
Third Edition, 1935
Fourth Edition, 1948
Fifth Edition, 1963; amended 1964;
Sixth Edition, 1979
Seventh Edition, 1988
Reprinted 1989
incorporating Amendment Sheets Nos 1 and 2
dated September 1988 and May 1989.
Reprinted 1992
incorporating Amendment Sheets Nos 1, 2 and 3
dated September 1988, May 1989 and May 1992.
Revised and Reprinted 1998
Reprinted 2000
incorporating Amendment Sheets Nos 1 and 2,
both dated 2000

Copyright   The Royal Institution of Chartered Surveyors
©1998   The Construction Confederation

ISBN 0 85406 360 9 (RICS)
ISBN 0 85263 004 3 (CC)

Designed and set by NBS Services Ltd, Newcastle upon Tyne
Re-set and printed by Thanet Press, Margate, Kent.

Summary of contents

To find the relevant work section for any given topic refer to the detailed contents list overleaf or to the alphabetical index.

Detailed contents Page 1

Alphabetical index

Detailed contents

* No specific rules included – see General rules clause 11.

H Cladding/Covering

H10	Patent glazing	71
H11	Curtain walling	72
H12	Plastics glazed vaulting/walling	71
H13	Structural glass assemblies	71
H14	Concrete rooflights/pavement lights	73
H20	Rigid sheet cladding	73
H21	Timber weatherboarding	73
H30	Fibre cement profiled sheet cladding/covering/siding	75
H31	Metal profiled sheet cladding/covering/siding	75
H32	Plastics profiled sheet cladding/covering/siding	75
H33	Bitumen and fibre profiled sheet cladding/covering	75
H40	Glassfibre reinforced cement panel cladding/features	53
H41	Glassfibre reinforced plastics panel cladding/features	75
H42	Precast concrete panel cladding/features	53
H43	Metal panel cladding/features	75
H50	Precast concrete slab cladding/features	53
H51	Natural stone slab cladding/features	77
H52	Cast stone slab cladding/features	77
H60	Plain roof tiling	79
H61	Fibre cement slating	79
H62	Natural slating	79
H63	Reconstructed stone slating/tiling	79
H64	Timber shingling	79
H65	Single lap roof tiling	79
H66	Bituminous felt shingling	79
H70	Malleable metal sheet prebonded coverings/cladding	80
H71	Lead sheet coverings/flashings	80
H72	Aluminium strip/sheet coverings/flashings	80
H73	Copper strip/sheet coverings/flashings	80
H74	Zinc strip/sheet coverings/flashings	80
H75	Stainless steel strip/sheet coverings/flashings	80
H76	Fibre bitumen thermoplastic sheet coverings/flashings	80
H90	Tensile fabric coverings	*
H91	Thatch roofing	*
H92	Rainscreen cladding	73

J Waterproofing

J10	Specialist waterproof rendering	103
J20	Mastic asphalt tanking/damp proofing	83
J21	Mastic asphalt roofing/insulation/finishes	83
J22	Proprietary roof decking with asphalt finish	83
J30	Liquid applied tanking/damp proofing	83
J31	Liquid applied waterproof roof coatings	83
J32	Sprayed vapour control layers	*
J33	In situ glassfibre reinforced plastics	*
J40	Flexible sheet tanking/damp proofing	85
J41	Built up felt roof coverings	85
J42	Single layer polymeric roof coverings	85
J43	Proprietary roof decking with felt finish	85
J44	Sheet linings for pools/lakes/waterways	85

K Linings/Sheathing/Dry partitioning

K10	Plasterboard dry linings/partitions/ceilings	87
K11	Rigid sheet flooring/sheathing/decking/sarking/linings/casings	73
K12	Under purlin/Inside rail panel linings	73
K13	Rigid sheet fine linings/panelling	73
K14	Glassfibre reinforced gypsum linings/panelling/casings/mouldings	73
K15	Vitreous enamel linings/panelling	73
K20	Timber board flooring/decking/sarking/linings/casings	73
K21	Timber strip/board fine flooring/linings	73
K30	Panel partitions	90
K32	Panel cubicles	91
K33	Concrete/Terrazzo partitions	53
K40	Demountable suspended ceilings	92
K41	Raised access floors	94

3

R Disposal systems

Code		
R10	Rainwater pipework/gutters	141
R11	Foul drainage above ground	141
R12	Drainage below ground	145
R13	Land drainage	145
R14	Laboratory/Industrial waste drainage	Y
R20	Sewage pumping	Y
R21	Sewage treatment/sterilisation	Y
R30	Centralised vacuum cleaning	Y
R31	Refuse chutes	Y
R32	Compactors/Macerators	Y
R33	Incineration plant	Y

S Piped supply systems

Code		
S10	Cold water	Y
S11	Hot water	Y
S12	Hot and cold water (self-contained specification)	Y
S13	Pressurised water	Y
S14	Irrigation	Y
S15	Fountains/Water features	Y
S20	Treated/Deionised/Distilled water	Y
S21	Swimming pool water treatment	Y
S30	Compressed air	Y
S31	Instrument air	Y
S32	Natural gas	Y
S33	Liquefied petroleum gas	Y
S34	Medical/Laboratory gas	Y
S40	Petrol/Diesel storage/distribution	Y
S41	Fuel oil storage/distribution	Y
S50	Vacuum	Y
S51	Steam	Y
S60	Fire hose reels	Y
S61	Dry risers	Y
S62	Wet risers	Y
S63	Sprinklers	Y
S64	Deluge	Y
S65	Fire hydrants	Y
S70	Gas fire fighting	Y
S71		Y

T Mechanical heating/Cooling/Refrigeration systems

Code		
T10	Gas/Oil fired boilers	Y
T11	Coal fired boilers	Y
T12	Electrode/Direct electric boilers	Y
T13	Packaged steam generators	Y
T14	Heat pumps	Y
T15	Solar collectors	Y
T16	Alternative fuel boilers	Y
T20	Primary heat distribution	Y
T30	Medium temperature hot water heating	Y
T31	Low temperature hot water heating	Y
T32	Low temperature hot water heating (self-contained specification)	Y
T33	Steam heating	Y
T40	Warm air heating	Y
T41	Warm air heating (self-contained specification)	Y
T42	Local heating units	Y
T50	Heat recovery	Y
T60	Central refrigeration plant	Y
T61	Chilled water	Y
T70	Local cooling units	Y
T71	Cold rooms	Y
T72	Ice pads	Y

U Ventilation/air conditioning systems

U10	General ventilation	Y
U11	Toilet ventilation	Y
U12	Kitchen ventilation	Y
U13	Car parking ventilation	Y
U14	Smoke extract/Smoke control	Y
U15	Safety cabinet/Fume cupboard extract	Y
U16	Fume extract	Y
U17	Anaesthetic gas extract	Y
U20	Dust collection	Y
U30	Low velocity air conditioning	Y
U31	VAV air conditioning	Y
U32	Dual-duct air conditioning	Y
U33	Multi-zone air conditioning	Y
U40	Induction air conditioning	Y
U41	Fan-coil air conditioning	Y
U42	Terminal re-heat air conditioning	Y
U43	Terminal heat pump air conditioning	Y
U50	Hybrid system air conditioning	Y
U60	Air conditioning units	Y
U70	Air curtains	Y

V Electrical supply/power/lighting systems

V10	Electricity generation plant	Y
V11	HV supply/distribution/public utility supply	Y
V12	LV supply/public utility supply	Y
V20	LV distribution	Y
V21	General lighting	Y
V22	General LV power	Y
V30	Extra low voltage supply	Y
V31	DC supply	Y
V32	Uninterruptable power supply	Y
V40	Emergency lighting	Y
V41	Street/Area/Flood lighting	Y
V42	Studio/Auditorium/Arena lighting	Y
V50	Electric underfloor/ceiling heating	Y
V51	Local electric heating units	Y
V90	Electrical installation (self-contained specification)	

W Communications/security/control systems

W10	Telecommunications	Y
W11	Paging/Emergency call	Y
W12	Public address/Conference audio facilities	Y
W20	Radio/TV/CCTV	Y
W21	Projection	Y
W22	Information/Advertising display	Y
W23	Clocks	Y
W30	Data transmission	Y
W40	Access control	Y
W41	Security detection and alarm	Y
W50	Fire detection and alarm	Y
W51	Earthing and bonding	Y
W52	Lightning protection	Y
W53	Electromagnetic screening	Y
W54	Liquid detection alarm	Y
W60	Central control/Building management	Y

X Transport Systems

X10	Lifts	149
X11	Escalators	149
X12	Moving pavements	149
X13	Powered stairlifts	149
X14	Fire escape chutes/slings	149
X20	Hoists	149
X21	Cranes	149
X22	Travelling cradles/gantries/ladders	149
X23	Goods distribution/Mechanised warehousing	149
X30	Mechanical document conveying	149
X31	Pneumatic document conveying	149
X32	Automatic document filing and retrieval	149

Y See Y Mechanical and electrical services measurement

7

Preface to First Edition 1922

For many years the Surveyors' Institution and the Quantity Surveyors' Association (which bodies are now amalgamated) were accepted as the recognised authorities for deciding disputed points in connection with the measurement of building works. The frequency of the demands upon their services for this purpose directed attention to the diversity of practice, varying with local custom, and even the idiosyncracies of individual surveyors, which obtained. This lack of uniformity afforded a just ground of complaint on the part of contractors that the estimator was frequently left in doubt as to the true meaning of items in the bills of quantities which he was called upon to price, a circumstance which militated against scientific and accurate tendering.

In the absence of any statutory qualifications for surveyors practising in the United Kingdom, any person, up to the present, has been at liberty to describe himself as a quantity surveyor, and the public have no guarantee that he is qualified for that office. This fact resulted in the issue of a considerable amount of unskilled work under the designation of bills of quantities.

Both the Surveyors' Institution and the Quantity Surveyors' Association were impressed with the necessity of securing greater accuracy of work and uniformity of method. The latter body, in July 1909, with this object in view appointed a Committee who prepared and published pamphlets setting out the method of measurement recommended by the Association in respect of three trades. The Surveyors' Institution also issued to its members circulars giving an authoritative opinion as to the correct method of measurement in the case of items in connection with which disputes had occurred. The

desirability of co-operation between the two societies thus became evident, and a Joint Committee was set up in June 1912, upon which was imposed the task of drawing up a comprehensive set of Standard Rules of Measurement of Building Works. In 1918 representatives of the building trades were added to this Committee, four contractors being nominated by the National Federation of Building Trades Employers and the Institute of Builders. The Joint Committee were assisted in their deliberations by interviews with the representatives of certain trades.

The Standard Method of Measurement of Building Works drawn up and set forth in the following pages is founded upon the practice of the leading London quantity surveyors with certain modifications by way of alternatives, and not involving matters of principle, to suit the practice obtaining in other parts of the Kingdom.

The Joint Committee was composed as follows: six surveyors nominated by the Surveyors' Institution and the Quantity Surveyors' Association, and four contractors nominated by the National Federation of Building Trades Employers and the Institute of Builders, viz. Surveyors: Messrs. F.A.H. Hardcastle (Chairman), Thomas E. Bare (Hon.Sec.), R.C. Gleed, Arnold E. Harris, Walter Lawrence, and Morgan H. Young. Contractors: Messrs. R. Friend (Rugby) (Vice-Chairman), W. Lacey (London), Stanley Miller (Newcastle-on-Tyne) and Frank Woods (Bolton, Lancashire).

Other gentlemen who have served on the Committee for a time are: Surveyors: Messrs. Arthur G. Cross, W.E. Davis, J.E. Drower, and Henry Riley. Contractor: Mr. Walter Lawrence (London).

Preface to Seventh Edition 1988

The Joint Working Party on Measurement Conventions set up by The Royal Institution of Chartered Surveyors and the then National Federation of Building Trades Employers reported in December 1971. Out of this report a Development Unit was set up and quickly came to the conclusion that far reaching changes were required. As an interim measure the Sixth Edition of the Standard Method of Measurement was published in March 1979. Now, with the publication of this Seventh Edition, the work envisaged by that working party has been completed.

The Co-ordinating Committee for Project Information has produced a Common Arrangement of Work Sections for Building Works. In support of the principles of CCPI and in accordance with the wishes of the sponsoring bodies, this Edition has been structured in common arrangement order rather than in traditional work sections. This means that the Standard Method of Measurement is now compatible with other CCPI publications and with all standard documentation where these criteria have been adopted. The other major change from previous editions is that the measurement rules have been translated from prose into classification tables. This change makes the use of the rules a quicker and more systematic task than interpretation of a prose version and readily lends itself to the use of standard phraseology and computerisation. The change however does not inhibit the use of traditional prose in the writing of bills of quantities if so desired. In addition to these two major changes, the rules have generally been simplified and the document brought up to date to equate wih modern practice.

The Committee expresses its thanks to the professional and trade associations for their co-operation and advice in the detailed consultations that have taken place and to the surveyors and builders who have assisted in testing the new rules, to Geoffrey E. Beard who chaired the Committee from June 1975 to September 1984 and especially to the editors who have had the task of bringing together all the various drafts and presenting them in a uniform manner in a relatively short space of time.

This Seventh Edition will become operative on 1 July 1988 and is post dated accordingly.

The Joint Committee responsible for this edition at the date of issue was composed as follows:

Appointed by the Royal Institution of Chartered Surveyors: Christopher J. Willis (Chairman), Ronald C. Allan, Keith W. Bailey, John Bennett, Eric J. Bowman, N. Malcolm S. Boyd, Michael A. Rainbird, Eric H. Urquhart and Michael J.T. Webb.

Appointed by the Building Employers Confederation: Andrew J. Costelloe (Vice-Chairman), John M. Allen, Bernard Ball, Kenneth G. Ellis, James E. Fisher, Colin M. Ford, Richard J. Hooker, Robert H. Inglis, Terence J. Parkinson and Donald J. Rimmer.

Co-opted from the Development Unit: Tony Allott, Stuart Hendy, Peter E. Holden, Peter G. Jordan and Rex H. Sharman.

Consultant Members of the Committee: Geoffrey E. Beard and Ian M.C. Hill.

Joint Honorary Secretaries: Norman R. Wheatley (General) and Michael B. Smith (Queries).

Others who have served on the Committee or the Development Unit during the preparation of this edition: Dr Martin Barnes, Robert A. Barrow, Ian T. Brown, Peter Graham, Alan M. Harrison, Patrick Kelly, Anthony R. Miller and Paul D. Morrell.

Consultant Editors appointed by the Committee: Paul J. Gilkes and Richard E.N. McGill

CJW: 1 October 1987

Preface to the Seventh Edition Revised

The Seventh Edition of the Standard Method of Measurement was published in 1988. Following experience in use and in consequence of queries raised minor amendments were made in September 1988, May 1989 and in May 1992. Now in 1998 further changes are required. The Seventh Edition when published was in a completely new format using as a base the Common Arrangement of Work Sections for Building Works as part of an initiative for Co-ordinated Project Information in the industry. In 1997 a further advancement in this initiative was made with the publication by the Construction Project Information Committee, the successors to the authors of the original CAWS, of a new manual entitled *UNICLASS*. *UNICLASS* is a document intended to be used for a wide number of different purposes including organising documents in libraries, project and cost information, specifications etc. Many potential users of *UNICLASS* are currently users of CAWS in one form or other. *UNICLASS* includes certain amendments to the original CAWS and as CAWS is the base document for SMM 7 it has been necessary to recognise these changes and to amend SMM 7. The changes are mainly to titling, phraseology and order and in consequence, whilst the changes incorporated in this revision are extensive, the changes to the rules themselves are minimal.

As well as making the changes consequent upon the amended CAWS the Standing Joint Committee have taken the opportunity to correct certain other anomalies that have arisen since the third amendment was published in 1992.

This Revised Seventh Edition will become operative on 3lst July 1998 and is postdated accordingly.

The Joint Committee responsible for this Amended Edition at the date of issue was composed as follows:

Appointed by the Royal Institution of Chartered Surveyors: Ronald C Allan (Chairman), Keith W. Bailey, Andrew O'Kelly, Michael A Rainbird, and Michael B.Smith.

Appointed by the Construction Confederation: Donald J Rimmer (Vice Chairman), Kevin M.Callan, Brian W.Gordon, and Richard J . Hooker.

Consultant members of the committee Andrew J.Costelloe and Christopher J Willis

Joint Honorary Secretaries: Norman R. Wheatley (General) and John D.O'N.Davidson (Queries).

RCA: 1 July 1998

General rules

1. Introduction

1.1

This Standard Method of Measurement provides a uniform basis for measuring building works and embodies the essentials of good practice. Bills of quantities shall fully describe and accurately represent the quantity and quality of the works to be carried out. More detailed information than is required by these rules shall be given where necessary in order to define the precise nature and extent of the required work.

1.2

The rules apply to measurement of proposed work and executed work.

2. Use of the tabulated rules

Generally

2.1

The rules in this document are set out in tables. Each section of the rules comprises information (to be) provided, classification tables and supplementary rules. The tabulated rules are written in the present tense.

2.2

Horizontal lines divide the classification table and supplementary rules into zones to which different rules apply.

Classification tables

2.3

Within the classification table where a broken line is shown, the rules given above and below the broken line may be used as alternatives.

2.4

In referring to columns in classification tables the measurement unit col-

2.5

The left hand column of the classification table lists descriptive features commonly encountered in building works. The next column lists further sub-groups into which each main group of items shall be divided and similarly the third column provides for further division. The lists in these columns are not intended to be exhaustive.

2.6

Each item description shall identify the work with respect to one descriptive feature drawn from each of the first three columns in the classification table and as many of the descriptive features in the fourth column as are applicable to the item. The general principle does not apply to Preliminaries in that it will be necessary to select as many descriptive features as appropriate from each column.

2.7

Where the abbreviation (nr) is given in the classification table the quantity shall be stated in the item description.

Supplementary rules

2.8

Within the supplementary rules everything above the horizontal line, which is immediately below the classification table heading, is applicable throughout that table.

2.9

Measurement rules set out when work shall be measured and the method by which quantities shall be computed.

2.10

Definition rules define the extent and limits of the work represented by a word or expression used in the rules and in a bill of quantities prepared in

2.11
Coverage rules draw attention to particular incidental work which shall be deemed to be included in the appropriate items in a bill of quantities to the extent that such work is included in the tender documents. Where the coverage rules include materials they shall be mentioned in the item descriptions.

2.12
The column headed Supplementary Information contains rules governing the information which shall be given in addition to the information given as a result of the application of rule 2.6.

2.13
A separate item shall be given for any work which differs from other work with respect to any matter listed as supplementary information.

3. Quantities

3.1
Work shall be measured net as fixed in position except where otherwise stated in a measurement rule applicable to the work.

3.2
Dimensions used in calculating quantities shall be taken to the nearest 10mm (i.e. 5mm and over shall be regarded as 10mm and less than 5mm shall be disregarded).

3.3
Quantities measured in tonnes shall be given to two places of decimals. Other quantities shall be given to the nearest whole unit except that any quantity less than one unit shall be given as one unit.

3.4
Unless otherwise stated, where minimum deductions for voids are dealt with in this document they shall refer only to openings or wants which are within the boundaries of measured areas. Openings or wants which are at the boundaries of measured areas shall always be the subject of deduction irrespective of size.

3.5
The requirement to measure separate items for widths not exceeding a stated limit shall not apply where these widths are caused by voids.

4. Descriptions

4.1
Dimensions shall be stated in descriptions generally in the sequence length, width, height. Where ambiguity could arise, the dimensions shall be identified.

4.2
Information required by the application of rules 2.6 and 2.12 may be given in documents (e.g. drawings or specification) separate from the bills of quantities if a precise and unique cross reference is given in its place in the description of the item concerned. This rule does not allow the aggregation of a number of measured items which are otherwise required to be measured separately by these rules, except as provided by rule 9.1.

4.3
Headings to groups of items in a bill of quantities shall be read as part of the descriptions of the items to which the headings apply.

4.4
The use of a hyphen between two dimensions in this document or in a bill of quantities shall mean a range of dimensions exceeding the first dimension stated but not exceeding the second.

4.5
Each work section of a bill of quantities shall begin with a description stating the nature and location of the work unless evident from the drawn or other information required to be provided by these rules.

4.6
Unless otherwise specifically stated in a bill of quantities or herein, the following shall be deemed to be included with all items:

(a) Labour and all costs in connection therewith.
(b) Materials, goods and all costs in connection therewith.
(c) Assembling, fitting and fixing materials and goods in position.
(d) Plant and all costs in connection therewith.
(e) Waste of materials.
(f) Square cutting.
(g) Establishment charges, overhead charges and profit.

4.7
A dimensioned description for an item in the bill of quantities shall define the item and state all the dimensions necessary to identify the shape and size of the item or its components.

(d) Work carried out in or under water shall be so described stating whether canal, river or sea water and (where applicable) the mean Spring levels of high and low water.

(e) Work carried out in compressed air shall be so described stating the pressure and the method of entry and exit.

8. Fixing, base and background

8.1

Method of fixing shall only be measured and described where required by the rules in each Work Section. Where fixing through vulnerable materials is required to be identified, such materials are deemed to include those listed in rule 8.3 (e).

8.2

Where the nature of the base is required to be identified each type of base shall be identified separately.

8.3

Where the nature of the background is required to be identified the item description shall state one of the following:

(a) Timber, which shall be deemed to include manufactured building boards.

(b) Masonry, which shall be deemed to include concrete, brick, block and stone.

(c) Metal.

(d) Metal faced materials.

(e) Vulnerable materials, which shall be deemed to include glass, marble, mosaic, tiled finishes and the like.

9. Composite items

9.1

Notwithstanding the requirement of clause 4.2, work to be manufactured off site may be combined into one item even though the rules require items to be measured separately, provided the items in question are all incorporated into the composite item off site. The item description shall identify the resulting composite item and the item shall be deemed to include breaking down for transport and installation and subsequent re-assembly.

5. Drawn information

5.1

Location drawings:

(a) Block Plan: shall identify the site and locate the outlines of the building works in relation to a town plan or other context.

(b) Site Plan: shall locate the position of the building works in relation to setting out points, means of access and general layout of the site.

(c) Plans, Sections and Elevations: shall show the position occupied by the various spaces in a building and the general construction and location of the principal elements.

5.2

Component drawings: shall show the information necessary for manufacture and assembly of a component.

5.3

Dimensioned diagrams: shall show the shape and dimensions of the work covered by an item and may be used in a bill of quantities in place of a dimensioned description, but not in place of an item otherwise required to be measured.

5.4

Schedules which provide the required information shall be deemed to be drawings as required under these rules.

6. Catalogued or standard components

6.1

A precise and unique cross-reference to a catalogue or to a standard specification may be given in an item description instead of the description required by rules 2.6 and 2.12 or instead of a component drawing.

7. Work of special types

7.1

Work of each of the following special types shall be separately identified:

(a) Work on or in an existing building – see general rule 13.

(b) Work to be carried out and subsequently removed (other than temporary works).

(c) Work outside the curtilage of the site.

10. Procedure where the drawn and specification information required by these rules is not available

10.1
Where work can be described and given in items in accordance with these rules but the quantity of work required cannot be accurately determined, an estimate of the quantity shall be given and identified as an approximate quantity.

10.2
Where work cannot be described and given in items in accordance with these rules it shall be given as a Provisional Sum and identified as for either defined or undefined work as appropriate.

10.3
A Provisional Sum for defined work is a sum provided for work which is not completely designed but for which the following information shall be provided:

(a) The nature and construction of the work.

(b) A statement of how and where the work is fixed to the building and what other work is to be fixed thereto.

(c) A quantity or quantities which indicate the scope and extent of the work.

(d) Any specific limitations and the like identified in Section A35.

10.4
Where Provisional Sums are given for defined work the Contractor will be deemed to have made due allowance in programming, planning and pricing Preliminaries. Any such allowance will only be subject to adjustment in those circumstances where a variation in respect of other work measured in detail in accordance with the rules would give rise to adjustment.

10.5
A Provisional Sum for undefined work is a sum provided for work where the information required in accordance with rule 10.3 cannot be given.

10.6
Where Provisional Sums are given for undefined work the Contractor will be deemed not to have made any allowance in programming, planning and pricing Preliminaries.

11. Work not covered

11.1
Rules of measurement adopted for work not covered by these rules shall be stated in a bill of quantities. Such rules shall, as far as possible, conform with those given in this document for similar work.

12. Symbols and abbreviations

12.1
The following symbols and abbreviations are used in this method of measurement:

m	=	metre
m²	=	square metre
m³	=	cubic metre
mm	=	millimetre
nr	=	number
kg	=	kilogramme
t	=	tonne
h	=	hour
pc sum	=	Prime Cost Sum
prov sum	=	Provisional Sum
>	=	exceeding
≥	=	equal to or exceeding
≤	=	not exceeding
<	=	less than
%	=	percentage
-	=	hyphen (see rule 4.4)

12.2
Cross references within the classification tables are given in the form:

Work Section number	Number from first column		Number from second column		Number from third column		Number from fourth column
		:		.		.	

Example:

D20:2. 2. 2. 1
Excavation and filling
   Excavating
      To reduce levels
         Maximum depth $\leq$ 1.00m
            Commencing level stated where $>$ 0.25m below existing ground level.

12.3
An asterisk within a cross reference represents all entries in the column in which it appears.

12.4
The digit 0 within a cross reference represents no entries in the column in which it appears.

13. Work to existing buildings

13.1
Work to existing buildings shall be so described. Such work is defined as work on, or in, or immediately under work existing before the current project.

13.2
The additional rules for work to existing buildings are to be read in conjunction with the preceding rules in the appropriate Work Sections.

13.3
A description of the additional Preliminaries/General conditions which are pertinent to the work to the existing building shall be given, drawing attention to any specific requirements due to the nature of the work.

14. General definitions

14.1
Where the rules require work to be described as curved with the radii stated details shall be given of the curved work including if concave or convex, if conical or spherical, if to more than one radius and shall state the radius or radii.

14.2
The radius stated shall be the mean radius measured to the centre line of the material unless otherwise stated.

A Preliminaries/General conditions

INFORMATION PROVIDED			MEASUREMENT RULES	DEFINITION RULES	COVERAGE RULES	SUPPLEMENTARY INFORMATION
P1 Location drawings as defined in General Rule 5.1 P2 Information to facilitate visiting site and addresses where drawings or other information additional to that required by these rules or other listed information may be inspected				D1 A fixed charge is for work the cost of which is to be considered as independent of duration D2 A time related charge is for work the cost of which is to be considered as dependent on duration	C1 Works of a temporary nature are deemed to include rates, fees and charges related thereto in Sections A36, A41, A42, and A44	
CLASSIFICATION TABLE						
A10 Project particulars						
1 Project particulars	1 Name, nature and location 2 Names and addresses of Employer and Consultants	item				
A11 Tender and contract documents						
1 Documents	1 List of drawings/other documents	1 Used for bill of quantities 2 To be used for contract	item			
A12 The site/Existing buildings						
1 The site/Existing buildings	1 Site boundaries 2 Existing buildings on or adjacent to the site 3 Existing mains/services 4 Others, details stated	item				
A13 Description of the Works						
1 Description of the work	1 Elements of each new building	item				
	2 Dimensions and shape relating to each building	1 Plan area and perimeter at each floor level 2 Heights between floors 3 Total height	M1 Given only when the equivalent information is not indicated on the drawings provided			

... headings of standard conditions

2 Special conditions or amendments to standard conditions

3 Appendix insertions

4 Employer's insurance responsibility

5 Performance guarantee bond/collateral warranties

A30 Employer's requirements: Tendering/Sub-letting/Supply

1 Employer's requirements or limitations	1 Details stated	1 Fixed charge 2 Time related charge	item

A31 Employer's requirements: Provision, content and use of documents

1 Employer's requirements or limitations	1 Details stated	1 Fixed charge 2 Time related charge	item

A32 Employer's requirements: Management of the Works

1 Employer's requirements or limitations	1 Details stated	1 Fixed charge 2 Time related charge	item

A33 Employer's requirements: Quality standards/control

1 Employer's requirements or limitations	1 Details stated	1 Fixed charge 2 Time related charge	item

A34 Employer's requirements: Security/Safety/Protection

1 Employer's requirements or limitations, details stated	1 Noise and pollution control 2 Maintain adjoining buildings 3 Maintain public and private roads 4 Maintain live services 5 Security 6 Protection of work in all sections 7 Others	1 Fixed charge 2 Time related charge	item

A Preliminaries/General conditions continued

CLASSIFICATION TABLE		MEASUREMENT RULES	DEFINITION RULES	COVERAGE RULES	SUPPLEMENTARY INFORMATION
A35 Employer's requirements: Specific limitations on method/sequence/timing/use of site					
1 Employer's requirements or limitations, details stated	1 Fixed charge — item 2 Time related charge 1 Design constraints 2 Method and sequence of work 3 Access 4 Use of the site 5 Use or disposal of materials found 6 Start of work 7 Working hours 8 Others				
A36 Employer's requirements: Facilities/Temporary works/Services					
1 Employer's requirements or limitations, details stated	1 Fixed charge — item 2 Time related charge 1 Offices 2 Sanitary accommodation 3 Temporary fences, hoardings, screens and roofs 4 Name boards 5 Technical and surveying equipment 6 Temperature and humidity 7 Telephone/Facsimile installation and rental/maintenance 8 Others 9 Telephone/Facsimile call charges — prov sum			C2 Heating, lighting, cleaning and maintenance are deemed to be included	
A37 Employer's requirements: Operation/Maintenance of the finished building					
1 Employer's requirements or limitations	1 Fixed charge — item 2 Time related charge				

2 Time related charge

includes management, trades supervision, engineering, programming and production, quantity surveying support staff and the like

A41 Contractor's general cost items: Site accommodation

1 Site accommodation	item	1 Fixed charge 2 Time related charge

D4 Site accommodation includes offices, laboratories, cabins, stores, compounds, canteens, sanitary facilities and the like

1 Made available by the Employer, details and conditions stated

A42 Contractor's general cost items: Services and facilities

1 Services and facilities	item	1 Fixed charge 2 Time related charge

1 Power
2 Lighting
3 Fuels
4 Water
5 Telephone and administration
6 Safety, health and welfare
7 Storage of materials
8 Rubbish disposal
9 Cleaning
10 Drying out
11 Protection of work in all sections
12 Security
13 Maintain public and private roads
14 Small plant and tools
15 Others

16 General attendance on nominated sub-contractors
17 General attendance of nominated sub-contractors in respect of the requirements of the Joint Fire Code

D5 Items listed are not exhaustive and are for convenience of pricing only

1 Made available by the Employer, details and conditions stated

C3 General attendance is deemed to include the use of the Contractor's temporary roads, pavings and paths, standing scaffolding, standing power operated hoisting plant, the provision of temporary lighting and water supplies, clearing away rubbish, provision of space for the sub-contractor's own offices and the storage of his plant and materials and the use of messrooms, sanitary accommodation and welfare facilities provided by the Contractor

C4 General attendance, where the Joint Fire Code applies is deemed to include hand bells, whistles, klaxons, manually operated sounders, security guards, fire signage (e.g. location of fire access routes and positions of dry riser inlets and fire extinguishers), fire doors and fire stopping to lift-shafts, service ducts and voids, water supplies for fire fighting equipment and the services of an appropriate number of Fire Marshalls where the works are a large project

A Preliminaries/General conditions continued

CLASSIFICATION TABLE				MEASUREMENT RULES	DEFINITION RULES	COVERAGE RULES	SUPPLEMENTARY INFORMATION
A43 Contractor's general cost items: Mechanical plant							
1 Mechanical plant	1 Cranes 2 Hoists 3 Personnel transport 4 Transport 5 Earthmoving plant 6 Concrete plant 7 Piling plant 8 Paving and surfacing plant 9 Others	item	1 Fixed charge 2 Time related charge	1 Made available by the Employer, details and conditions stated			
					D6 Items listed are not exhaustiive and are for convenience of pricing only		
A44 Contractor's general cost items: Temporary works							
1 Temporary works	1 Temporary roads 2 Temporary walkways 3 Access scaffolding 4 Support scaffolding and propping 5 Hoardings, fans, fencing etc. 6 Hardstanding 7 Traffic regulations 8 Others	item	1 Fixed charge 2 Time related charge	1 Made available by the Employer, details and conditions stated			
					D7 Items listed are not exhaustive and are for convenience of pricing only		
A50 Work/Products by/on behalf of the Employer							
1 Work/Materials by the Employer	1 Work by others directly employed by the Employer, details stated 2 Attendance on others directly employed by the Employer, details stated 3 Materials provided by or on behalf of the Employer, details stated	item					

First	Second	Third	Unit	Measurement / Definition / Coverage / Supplementary rules
	2 Main contractor's profit		%	
	3 Special attendance, details stated	1 Scaffolding 2 Access roads 3 Hardstandings 4 Positioning 5 Storage 6 Power 7 Temperature and humidity 8 Others	item	**Rule 10.3** 1 Fixed charge 2 Time related charge

Rules (upper section):

measured in Section A42

D8 Scaffolding under this rule is special scaffolding, scaffolding additional to the Contractor's standing scaffolding, or standing scaffolding required to be altered or retained

D9 Positioning includes unloading, distributing, hoisting and placing in position giving in the case of significant items the weight and/or size and position relative to ground level or other datum

S1 Particulars of any costs to be paid of conveying goods and materials to the site and/or of any special packing or similar requirements

A52 Nominated suppliers

First	Second	Third	Unit	Rules
1 Nominated suppliers	1 Supplier's materials	1 Description stated	p c sum	M3 Fixing only such items is measured in the appropriate Work Section
	2 Main contractor's profit		%	

C5 Fixing only such items is deemed to include unloading, storing, hoisting the goods and materials and returning packaging materials to the nominated supplier carriage paid and obtaining credits therefor

A53 Work by statutory authorities/undertakers

First	Second	Third	Unit	Rules
1 Work by statutory authorities	1 Work by the local authority		prov sum	D10 Work by statutory authorities includes work by public companies responsible for statutory work when executing their statutory duty
	2 Work by statutory undertakers			

A54 Provisional work

First	Second	Third	Unit	Rules
1 Provisional work	1 Defined		prov sum	D11 For defined and undefined provisional sums see General Rule 10
	2 Undefined			

A55 Dayworks

First	Second	Third	Unit	Rules
1 Dayworks	1 Labour		prov sum	
	2 Materials			
	3 Plant			

C Existing site/buildings/services

C20 Demolition

C21 Toxic/Hazardous material removal

C30 Shoring/Facade retention

INFORMATION PROVIDED

P1 The following information is shown either on location drawings under A Preliminaries/General conditions or on further drawings which accompany the bills of quantities:

(a) the location and extent of existing structures to be demolished

CLASSIFICATION TABLE

Classification			MEASUREMENT RULES	DEFINITION RULES	COVERAGE RULES	SUPPLEMENTARY INFORMATION
			M1 The rules within this Section apply to works to existing buildings as defined in the General Rules			
1 Demolishing all structures 2 Demolishing individual structures 3 Demolishing parts of structures	1 Levels to which structures are demolished	item 1 Materials remaining the property of the Employer 2 Materials for re-use 3 Making good structures 4 Leaving parts of existing walls temporarily in position to act as buttresses 5 Temporarily diverting, maintaining or sealing off existing services 6 Toxic/hazardous material, type stated	M2 Only temporarily diverting, maintaining or sealing off existing services is measured under this rule	D1 Materials arising from demolitions are the property of the Contractor unless otherwise stated D2 Demolishing parts of structures excludes items covered by Section C90 D3 Toxic/Hazardous material defined as Section D20 Rule D3	C1 Demolition items are deemed to include: (a) disposal of materials other than those remaining the property of the Employer or those for re-use (b) temporary support incidental to demolitions which is at the discretion of the Contractor	S1 Method of demolition where by specific means S2 Setting aside and storing materials remaining the property of the Employer or those for re-use S3 Employer's restrictions on methods of disposal of materials
4 Support of structures not to be demolished 5 Support of roads and the like	1 Position and type of shoring and nature of structure or road to be shored stated	item 1 Providing and erecting 2 Maintaining, duration stated 3 Adapting, details stated 4 Clearing away 5 Cutting holes in the structure, details stated 6 Making good all work disturbed		D4 Support is other than temporary support incidental to demolitions	C2 Support is deemed to include nails, wedges and bolts	

3	Adapting, details stated
4	Clearing away
5	Disposing of rainwater, details stated
6	Providing openings, details stated

C40 Cleaning masonry/concrete
C41 Repairing/Renovating/Conserving masonry
C42 Repairing/Renovating/Conserving concrete

	MEASUREMENT RULES	DEFINITION RULES	COVERAGE RULES	SUPPLEMENTARY INFORMATION
INFORMATION PROVIDED P1 The following information is shown either on location drawings under A Preliminaries/General conditions or on further drawings which accompany the bills of quantities: (a) the scope and location of the work relative to the existing layout indicating the existing structure	M1 The rules within this Section apply to works to existing buildings as defined in the General Rules	D1 Materials arising are the property of the Contractor unless otherwise stated D2 Locations stated relative to the existing building	C1 Shoring and scaffolding incidental to the work and making good all work disturbed by such shoring and scaffolding is deemed to be included C2 Work to existing buildings items are deemed to include: (a) disposal of materials other than those remaining the property of the Employer or those for re-use (b) incidental work which is at the discretion of the Contractor (c) all new fixing or joining materials required	S1 Method of operation, where by specific means S2 Setting aside and storing materials remaining the property of the Employer or those for re-use S3 Employer's restrictions on methods of disposal of materials S4 Restrictions on the method of shoring and scaffolding

CLASSIFICATION TABLE

					MEASUREMENT RULES	DEFINITION RULES	COVERAGE RULES	SUPPLEMENTARY INFORMATION
1 Cutting out defective concrete and replacing with new	1 Dimensioned description	1 Plain, details stated 2 Reinforced, details stated 3 Gun applied, details stated	m² m nr	1 Treatment of reinforcement, details stated 2 Anchored mesh reinforcement, details stated			C3 Formwork and making good to match existing are deemed to be included	S5 Method of bonding new to existing
2 Resin or cement impregnation/injection	1 Dimensioned description	1 Concrete, details stated 2 Brickwork, details stated 3 Blockwork, details stated 4 Stonework, details stated	m² m nr	1 Centres of drilling holes 2 Removing existing finishes			C4 Work is deemed to include making good holes and finishes on completion	
3 Cutting out decayed, defective or cracked work and replacing with new	1 Size and depth or thickness stated	1 Brickwork, details stated 2 Blockwork, details stated 3 Stonework, details stated	m² m nr	1 Making good with materials other than to match existing, details stated			C5 Work is deemed to include making good to match existing	S6 Method of bonding new to existing
4 Repointing	1 Size and depth of raking out of existing joint	1 Brickwork, details stated 2 Blockwork, details stated 3 Stonework, details stated	m² m nr	1 Type of pointing	M2 Details stated include bond and size of component		C6 Repointing is deemed to include making good to adjoining work	S7 Composition and mix of mortar

CLASSIFICATION TABLE

				Unit		MEASUREMENT RULES	DEFINITION RULES	COVERAGE RULES	SUPPLEMENTARY INFORMATION
5 Removing stains and the like (nr)	1 > 1.00 m² 2 ≤ 1.00 m²	1 Concrete 2 Brickwork 3 Blockwork 4 Stonework	1 Facings 2 Efflorescence 3 Stains 4 Graffiti 5 Vegetation 6 Algae 7 Others, details stated	m² nr		M3 Number of areas is only stated in the description when measured in m²			S8 Special cleaning materials
6 Cleaning surfaces	1 Concrete 2 Brickwork 3 Blockwork 4 Stonework	1 Facings	1 Washing 2 Abrasive blasting 3 Chemical treatments 4 Others, details stated	m²					S9 Cleaning materials
7 Inserting new wall ties	1 Size and type of tie	1 Brickwork 2 Blockwork 3 Stonework	1 Surface finishes, details stated	nr		M4 Inserting new wall ties is measured here only when executed without demolition			
8 Re-dressing to new profile	1 Detailed description and size of new profile 2 Detailed description and length and size of new profile			m nr		M5 Work is measured linear where of a continuous nature			
9 Artificial weathering	1 Concrete 2 Brickwork 3 Blockwork 4 Stonework	1 To match existing		m²					S10 Details of cutting away and making good

C45 Damp proof course renewal/insertion

INFORMATION PROVIDED			MEASUREMENT RULES	DEFINITION RULES	COVERAGE RULES	SUPPLEMENTARY INFORMATION
P1 The following information is shown either on location drawings under A Preliminaries/General conditions or on further drawings which accompany the bills of quantities: (a) the scope and location of the work relative to the existing layout indicating the existing structure					C1 Works are deemed to include: (a) disposal of materials (b) making good to holes and finishes after injection	S1 Method of operation, where by specific means S2 Damp proof chemicals
CLASSIFICATION TABLE						
1 Chemical damp proof courses 2 Injection mortar damp proof courses 3 Inserted mechanical damp proof courses	1 Brickwork 2 Blockwork 3 Stonework	m	1 Thickness of wall stated	1 Centres of drilling holes 2 Removing existing finishes		

C50 Repairing/Renovating/Conserving metal
C51 Repairing/Renovating/Conserving timber
C52 Fungus/Beetle eradication

INFORMATION PROVIDED			MEASUREMENT RULES	DEFINITION RULES	COVERAGE RULES	SUPPLEMENTARY INFORMATION
P1 The following information is shown either on location drawings under A Preliminaries/General conditions or on further drawings which accompany the bills of quantities: (a) the scope and location of the work						
CLASSIFICATION TABLE						
1 Repairing metal 2 Repairing timber	1 Dimensioned description	m² m nr	M1 The dimensioned description or dimensioned diagram (in conjunction with the Information Provided) must clearly identify all work in exploration, preparation and execution together with the associated works	D1 Repairing includes renovation, conservation or refurbishment		S1 Such information as is appropriate to the repair, renovation or refurbishment of the item
3 Treating existing timber						S2 Such information as is appropriate to the treatment

INFORMATION PROVIDED		MEASUREMENT RULES	DEFINITION RULES	COVERAGE RULES	SUPPLEMENTARY INFORMATION
P1 The following information is shown either on location drawings under A Preliminaries/General conditions or on further drawings which accompany the bills of quantities: (a) the scope and location of the work relative to the existing layout indicating the existing structure		M1 The rules within this Section apply to works to existing buildings as defined in the General Rules M2 Any operation to existing buildings involving removal of existing materials (other than for bonding purposes or renewal) is measured within this Section	D1 Materials arising from alterations - spot items are the property of the Contractor unless otherwise stated D2 Location is stated relative to existing building	C1 Shoring and scaffolding incidental to the work and making good all work disturbed by such shoring and scaffolding is deemed to be included within each item C2 Alterations - spot items are deemed to include: (a) disposal of materials other than those remaining the property of the Employer or those for re-use (b) work incidental to alterations - spot items which is at the discretion of the Contractor (c) all new fixing or joining materials required	S1 Method of operation, where by specific means S2 Setting aside and storing materials remaining the property of the Employer or those for re-use S3 Employer's restrictions on methods of disposal of materials S4 Employer's restrictions on methods of shoring and scaffolding to be used

CLASSIFICATION TABLE

			MEASUREMENT RULES	DEFINITION RULES	COVERAGE RULES	SUPPLEMENTARY INFORMATION
1 Removing fittings and fixtures 2 Removing plumbing and engineering installations 3 Removing finishings 4 Removing coverings 5 Cutting openings or recesses 6 Cutting back projections 7 Cutting to reduce thickness 8 Filling in openings	1 Details sufficient for identification stated 2 Dimensioned description sufficient for identification including type and thickness of existing structure	item				
		1 Making good structures 2 Extending and making good finishings 3 Inserting new work, details stated 4 Toxic/Hazardous material, type stated	M3 Details stated for inserting new work are the equivalent of those details required by the rules for the measurement of the same in other work sections	D3 Inserting new work includes re-fixing or re-using removed materials D4 Toxic/Hazardous material defined as Section D20 Rule D3		
9 Temporary roofs 10 Temporary screens	1 Dimensioned description	item				
		1 Providing and erecting 2 Maintaining, duration stated 3 Adapting, details stated 4 Clearing away 5 Disposing of rainwater, details stated 6 Providing openings, details stated				S5 Details of weather and dust proofing requirements

D Groundwork

D20 Excavating and filling
Q20 Granular sub-bases to roads/pavings

INFORMATION PROVIDED

P1 The following information is shown either on location drawings under A Preliminaries/General conditions or on further drawings which accompany the bills of quantities or stated as assumed:

(a) the ground water level and the date when it was established, defined as the pre-contract water level

(b) the ground water level is to be re-established at the time each excavation is carried out and is defined as the post contract water level

(c) ground water levels subject to periodic changes due to tidal or similar effects are so described giving the mean high and low water levels

(d) details of trial pits or boreholes including their location

(e) features retained

(f) live over or underground services indicating location

(g) pile sizes and layout in accordance with Sections D30 – D32 where applicable

CLASSIFICATION TABLE

		Unit	MEASUREMENT RULES	DEFINITION RULES	COVERAGE RULES	SUPPLEMENTARY INFORMATION

1 Site preparation	1 Removing trees
	  1 Girth 600 mm – 1.50 m
	  2 Girth 1.50 – 3.00 m
	  3 Girth > 3.00 m, girth stated
	2 Removing tree stumps
		nr	M1 Tree girths are measured at a height of 1.00 m above ground
			M2 Stump girths are measured at the top
					C1 This work is deemed to include:
					(a) grubbing up roots
					(b) disposal of materials
					(c) filling voids
						S1 Filling material described

	3 Clearing site vegetation 4 Description sufficient for identification stated	m²		D1 Site vegetation is bushes, scrub, undergrowth, hedges and trees and tree stumps ≤ 600 mm girth		
	4 Lifting turf for preservation 1 Method of preserving, details stated	m²				

				Measurement Rules	Definition Rules	Coverage Rules	Supplementary Information
	2 Maximum depth ≤ 1.00 m 3 Maximum depth ≤ 2.00 m 4 and thereafter in 2.00 m stages			for subsequent variations to bulk or for extra space for working space or to accommodate earthwork support M4 Excavating for ground beams not between piles is measured under 2.5 & 6.*.**	gas only or *... to pollute ground water* D3 Toxic/hazardous material is active material where precautions are specifically required		
	3 Basements and the like 4 Pits (nr) 5 Trenches, width ≤ 0.30 m 6 Trenches, width > 0.30 m 7 For pile caps and ground beams between piles 8 To bench sloping ground to receive filling						
3 Items extra over any types of excavating irrespective of depth	1 Excavating below ground water level		m³	M5 If the post contract water level differs from the pre-contract water level the measurements are revised accordingly			S2 Nature of special requirement
	2 Active material						
	3 Toxic/hazardous material, type stated				D4 Retaining a service is a precaution specifically required		
	4 Next existing services	1 Type of service stated	m	M6 To be measured where precautions are specifically required			
	5 Around existing services crossing excavation		nr				
4 Breaking out existing materials	1 Rock 2 Concrete	1 Extra over any types of excavating irrespective of depth	m³		D5 Rock is any material which is of such size or position that it can only be removed by wedges, special plant or explosives		
5 Breaking out existing hard pavings, thickness stated	3 Reinforced concrete 4 Brickwork, blockwork or stonework 5 Coated macadam or asphalt		m²				
6 Working space allowance to excavations	1 Reduce levels, basements and the like 2 Pits 3 Trenches 4 Pile caps and ground beams between piles		m²	M7 Working space is measured where the face of the excavation is < 600 mm from the face of formwork, rendering, tanking or protective walls M8 The area measured is calculated by multiplying the girth of the formwork, rendering, tanking or protective walls by the depth of excavation below the commencing level of the excavation	D6 Backfilling with special materials occurs where selected or treated excavated materials or imported materials are used	C2 Additional earthwork support, disposal, backfilling, work below ground water level and breaking out are deemed to be included	S3 Details of backfilling with special materials

D20 Q20 continued

CLASSIFICATION TABLE				MEASUREMENT RULES	DEFINITION RULES	COVERAGE RULES	SUPPLEMENTARY INFORMATION
7 Earthwork support	1 Maximum depth ≤ 1.00 m 2 Maximum depth ≤ 2.00 m 3 and thereafter in 2.00 m stages	m²	1 Curved 2 Below ground water level 3 Unstable ground 4 Next to roadways 5 Next to existing buildings 6 Left in	M9 Earthwork support is measured the full depth to all faces of excavation whether or not required except to: (a) face ≤ 0.25 m high (b) sloping faces of excavations where the angle of inclination is ≤ 45° from the horizontal (c) faces of excavations which abut existing walls, piers, or other structures M10 Earthwork support below ground water level or in unstable ground is measured from the commencing level of the excavation to the full depth M11 Earthwork support below ground water level is only measured where a corresponding item is measured in accordance with 3.1.0.0 and is adjusted accordingly if the post contract water level is different	D7 Earthwork support is deemed to mean providing everything to uphold the sides of excavation by means other than interlocking steel piling which is measured in Section D32 D8 Earthwork support next to roadways occurs where the horizontal distance from the face supported to the edge of the roadway or footpath is < the depth of the excavated face below the bottom of the foundations D9 Earthwork support next to existing buildings occurs where the horizontal distance from the face supported to the nearest part of the foundations of the building, is < the depth of the excavated face below the bottom of the foundations D10 Unstable ground is running silt, running sand, loose gravel and the like	C3 Curved earthwork support is deemed to include any extra costs of curved excavation	
8 Disposal		item	1 Surface water 2 Ground water	M12 An item for disposal of ground water is only measured where a corresponding item is measured in accordance with 3.1, and is adjusted accordingly if the post contract water level is different	D11 Surface water is water on the surface of site and the excavations		
	3 Excavated material	m³	1 Off site 2 On site	M13 The quantity given for disposal is the bulk before excavating and no allowance is made for subsequent variations to bulk or for extra space to accommodate earthwork support		C4 Any type of excavated or broken out material is deemed to be included	
			1 Specified locations, details stated 2 Specified handling, details stated 3 Active material 4 Toxic/hazardous material,				

			Unit				
11 Filling to external planters and the like, position stated	2 Average thickness > 0.25 m	2 Obtained from on site spoil heaps 3 Obtained off site, type stated		3 Topsoil 4 Specified handling, details stated	M15 The average thickness measured for filling is that after compaction M16 The position of external planters and the like is only stated where not at ground level		S5 Method of filling and compacting in layers
12 Surface packing to filling	1 To vertical or battered faces		m²		D12 Work is only described as battered where the slope > 15° from horizontal		
13 Surface treatments	1 Applying herbicides		m²		M17 Surface treatments may alternatively be given in the description of any superficial item		S6 Kind and quality of materials and rate of application
	2 Compacting	1 Ground 2 Filling 3 Bottoms of excavations		1 Blinding, material stated	M18 Specific blinding beds are measured as filling 10.*.*.* M19 Concrete blinding beds are measured in Section E10	C5 Compacting is deemed to include levelling and grading to falls and slopes ≤ 15° from horizontal	S7 Method of compacting S8 Kind and quality of materials
	3 Trimming	1 Sloping surfaces		1 In rock	M20 Trimming sloping surfaces is only measured where the slope is > 15° from horizontal		
		2 Sides of cuttings 3 Sides of embankments		1 Battered 2 Vertical 3 In rock			
	4 Trimming rock to produce fair or exposed face						
	5 Preparing subsoil for top soil						S9 Method of preparing

D30 Piling

INFORMATION PROVIDED	MEASUREMENT RULES	DEFINITION RULES	COVERAGE RULES	SUPPLEMENTARY INFORMATION
P1 The following information is shown either on location drawings under A Preliminaries/General conditions or on further drawings which accompany the bills of quantities: (a) the general piling layout (b) the positions of different types of piles (c) the positions of the work within the site and of existing services (d) the relationship to adjacent buildings P2 Soil description: (a) the nature of the ground is given in accordance with Section D20 Information Provided (b) where work is carried out near canals, rivers, etc. or tidal waters, the level of the ground in relation to the normal levels of the canal or river etc. or to the mean Spring levels of high and low tidal waters, is stated; flood levels are stated where applicable P3 Commencing levels: (a) the levels from which the work is expected to begin and from which measurements have been taken are stated; irregular ground is so described				S1 Kind and quality of materials and mix details S2 Tests of materials S3 Type of grout S4 Details of compaction

CLASSIFICATION TABLE
CAST IN PLACE CONCRETE PILING

					MEASUREMENT RULES	DEFINITION RULES	COVERAGE RULES
1 Bored piles 2 Driven shell piles	1 Nominal diameter stated	nr	1 Total number, commencing surface stated	1 Preliminary piles 2 Contiguous bored piles 3 Secant piles 4 Raking, inclination ratio stated	M1 Bored and driven lengths are measured along the axes of the piles from the commencing surface to the bottom of the shafts of bored piles and to the bottom of the casings of driven piles	D1 Piles comprising a driven light gauge casing which is first filled with concrete and then withdrawn are classed as driven shell piles where the piles are designed for the load to be carried on the concrete	C1 Total concrete length is deemed to include concrete placed in excess of the completed length
		m	2 Total concreted length			D2 Filling such piles is not classed as filling hollow piles in accordance with Section D30.20.1**	C2 Pre-boring is deemed to include grouting up voids between sides of piles and bores
		m	3 Total bored or driven length, maximum length stated				
3 Pre-boring driven piles		m	1 Maximum depth stated		M2 Pre-boring is only measured where it is specifically required		
4 Backfilling empty bores		m	1 Type of backfill material stated				
5 Items extra over piling	1 Breaking through obstructions	h			M3 Breaking through obstructions is only measured where obstructions are encountered above the founding stratum of the pile		
	2 Enlarging bases for bored piles 3 Enlarging bases for driven shell piles	nr	1 Diameter of enlarged base stated				C3 The work is deemed to include work below the specified bottom

First Division	Second Division	Third Division	Unit	Measurement Rules	Definition Rules	Coverage Rules	Additional Description Rules
		2 Length > 13 m (nr)		commencing surface		heads and shoes	S6 Details of driving heads and shoes where not at the discretion of the Contractor
7 Cutting off tops of piles (nr)	1 Nominal diameter stated	1 Total length 1 Tops of permanent casings	m			C5 Cutting off tops of piles is deemed to include preparation and integration of reinforcement into pile cap or ground beam and disposal	
8 Reinforcement to piles	1 Nominal size of bars stated 2 Nominal size of helical bars stated	1 Nominal diameter of piles stated	t			C6 Reinforcement to piles is deemed to include tying wire, spacers, links and binders which are at the discretion of the Contractor	S7 Kind and quality of materials
9 Disposal	1 Excavated materials	1 Off site 2 On site 1 Specified locations, details stated 2 Specified handling, details stated 3 Active material 4 Toxic/hazardous material, type stated	m³	M6 The volume of disposal of surplus excavated materials is calculated from the nominal cross-sectional size of piles and their lengths measured in accordance with 1 & 2.1.2.* The volume of enlarged bases is added to this calculation	D3 Active, toxic/hazardous material as defined Section D20 Rules D2 and D3		
10 Delays	1 Rig standing		h	M7 Delays are only measured where specifically authorised		C7 Delays are deemed to include associated labour	
11 Pile tests	1 Details stated		nr				S8 Timing and details of tests

35

D30 continued

CLASSIFICATION TABLE
PREFORMED CONCRETE PILING

Classification		Unit	MEASUREMENT RULES	DEFINITION RULES	COVERAGE RULES	SUPPLEMENTARY INFORMATION
12 Reinforced piles 13 Prestressed piles 14 Reinforced sheet piles 15 Hollow section piles 16 Reinforced segmental piles	1 Nominal cross-sectional size stated		1 Preliminary piles 2 Raking, inclination stated	nr	M8 The measurement for the total driven depth includes for driving extended piles	D4 The total driven depth is that specifically required by the designer	C8 Driving heads and shoes are deemed to be included	S9 Kind and quality of materials S10 Tests of materials S11 Details of driving heads and shoes
		2 Total driven depth	m	M9 The driven depth is measured from the commencing surface to the bottom of the pile toe along the axis of the pile			
17 Items extra over piling		1 Redriving piles	nr	M10 Redriving piles is only measured where it is specifically required			
18 Pre-boring		1 Maximum depth stated	m	M11 Pre-boring is only measured where it is specifically required		C9 Pre-boring is deemed to include grouting up voids between sides of piles and bores	S12 Type of grout
19 Jetting							
20 Filling hollow piles with concrete		1 Plain 2 Reinforced, details stated	m m				S13 Specification of concrete and reinforcement
21 Pile extensions		1 Total number 2 Extension length ≤ 3.00 m 3 Extension length > 3.00 m	nr m m			C10 Preparing heads, to receive pile extensions is deemed to be included	
22 Cutting off tops of piles (nr)		1 Total length	m			C11 Cutting off tops of piles is deemed to include prepration and integration of reinforcement into pile cap or ground beam and disposal	
23 Disposal	1 Excavated material	1 Off site 2 On site	m³	1 Special locations, details stated 2 Specified handling, details stated 3 Active material 4 Toxic/hazardous material, type stated	M12 The volume of disposal of surplus excavated materials is calculated from the nominal cross-sectional size of piles and their depths measured in accordance with 12–16.1.1 and 2.*	D5 Active, toxic/hazardous material as defined Section D20 Rules D2 and D3	
24 Delays	1 Rig standing		h	M13 Delays are only measured where they are specifically authorised			C12 Delays are deemed to include associated labour

CLASSIFICATION TABLE
STEEL PILING

					MEASUREMENT RULES	DEFINITION RULES	COVERAGE RULES	SUPPLEMENTARY INFORMATION
26 Isolated piles	1 Mass per metre and cross-sectional size, or section reference stated	nr	1 Total number driven specified length and commencing surface stated	1 Preliminary piles 2 Raking, inclination ratio stated	M14 The measurement of the total driven depths includes for driving extended piles M15 The driven depth is measured from the commencing surface to the bottom of the pile toe along the axis of the pile	D6 The specified length is that specifically required by the designer	C13 The cost of extraction is deemed to be included with piles so described	S15 Kind and quality of materials S16 Tests of materials
		m	2 Total driven depth	3 To be extracted				
27 Interlocking piles	1 Section modulus and cross-sectional size, or section reference stated	m²	1 Total area of specified length ≤ 14.00 m 2 Total area of specified length 14.00 – 24.00 m 3 Total area of specified length > 24.00 m		M16 The following separate items are required for each group of interlocking piles: (a) one or more items for the total area of the group of piles divided into the ranges of specified lengths given in 27.1.1–3.* (b) an item for the total driven area of the group of piles M17 The areas of items for interlocking piles are calculated by multiplying the mean undeveloped horizontal lengths of the pile walls formed (including lengths occupied by special piles) by the depths measured in accordance with the defintions of driven depths in the case of items for the driven areas and by the lengths measured in accordance with the definition of lengths in the case of items for the specified areas of piles			
			4 Total driven area					

D30 continued

CLASSIFICATION TABLE

Classification Table			Unit		MEASUREMENT RULES	DEFINITION RULES	COVERAGE RULES	SUPPLEMENTARY INFORMATION
28 Items extra over interlocking piles	1 Corners 2 Junctions 3 Closures 4 Tapers	1 Type stated	m		M18 The length measured for items extra over is the total length			
29 Isolated pile extensions	1 Mass per metre and cross-sectional size, or section reference stated	1 Total number	nr	1 Preliminary piles 2 Raking, inclination ratio stated	M19 Separate items are required for the length of pile extensions and for the number of pile extensions		C14 The cost of extraction is deemed to be included with piles so described	
		2 Extension length ≤ 3.00m	m					
	2 Section modulus and cross-sectional size, or section reference stated	3 Extension length > 3.00m		3 To be extracted 4 Using materials arising from cutting off surplus lengths of other piles			C15 Pile extensions are deemed to include the work necessary to attach the extension to the pile	
30 Interlocking pile extensions	1 Mass per metre and cross-sectional size, or section reference stated			1 Preliminary piles 2 Raking, inclination ratio stated				
	2 Section modulus and cross-sectional size, or section reference stated							
31 Cutting off surplus from specified lengths	1 Mass per metre and cross-sectional size, or section reference stated	1 Isolated piles (nr)	m		M20 The length measured is the surplus length of each pile		C16 Cutting off surplus from specified lengths of piles is deemed to include provision and filling of working space and disposal	
	2 Section modulus and cross-sectional size, or section reference stated	2 Interlocking piles (nr)	m					
32 Cutting interlocking piles to form holes	1 Dimensioned description		nr					
33 Delays	1 Rig standing	1 Isolated piles	h		M21 Delays are only measured where specifically authorised		C17 Delays are deemed to include associated labour	
		2 Interlocking piles						
34 Pile tests	1 Details stated		nr					S17 Timing and details of tests

D40 Embedded retaining walls

INFORMATION PROVIDED

P1 The following information is shown either on location drawings under A Preliminaries/General conditions or on further drawings which accompany the bills of quantities:
(a) the arrangement of embedded retaining walls and their relationship to surrounding buildings
(b) the depths, lengths and thicknesses of embedded retaining walls

P2 Soil description:
(a) the nature of the ground is given in accordance with Section D20 Information Provided
(b) where work is carried out near canals, rivers, etc. or tidal waters, the level of the ground in relation to the normal level of the canal or river etc. or to the mean Spring levels of high and low tidal waters is stated; flood levels are stated where applicable

P3 Commencing levels:
(a) the levels from which the work is expected to begin and from which measurements have been taken are stated
(b) irregular ground is so described

CLASSIFICATION TABLE
DIAPHRAGM WALLING

					MEASUREMENT RULES	DEFINITION RULES	COVERAGE RULES	SUPPLEMENTARY INFORMATION
1 Excavation and disposal	1 Thickness of wall stated		1 Maximum depth stated	m³	**M1** Piled walls are measured in accordance with Section D30			
					M2 The volume of excavation and disposal is calculated using the nominal lengths and depths of the walls. The depths are taken from the commencing surface			**S1** Details of support fluid **S2** Limitations on method of disposal
2 Items extra over excavation and disposal	1 Active material			m³		**D1** Active, toxic/hazardous material as defined Section D20 Rules D2 and D3		
	2 Toxic/hazardous material, type stated							
	3 Breaking out existing materials	1 Rock						
		2 Concrete						
		3 Reinforced concrete						
		4 Brickwork, blockwork or stonework						
		5 Coated macadam or asphalt						
	4 Breaking out existing hard pavings, thickness stated			m²				
3 Backfilling empty trench	1 Type of fill material stated			m³				
4 Concrete	1 Thickness of wall stated			m³	**M3** Concrete volume is measured net except that deductions are not made for the following: (a) reinforcement (b) steel sections of areas ≤ 0.50 m² (c) cast in accessories (d) voids ≤ 0.05 m³ in volume			**S3** Materials and mix details **S4** Tests

CLASSIFICATION TABLE				MEASUREMENT RULES	DEFINITION RULES	COVERAGE RULES	SUPPLEMENTARY INFORMATION
5 Reinforcement				M4 Reinforcement is measured in accordance with Section E30 and the mass measured includes that of stiffening, lifting and supporting steel cast in where specifically required			
6 Cutting off to specified level	1 Thickness of wall stated		m			C1 Cutting off to specified level is deemed to include provision and filling of working space and disposal	
7 Trimming and cleaning face of diaphragm walling	1 Details stated		m²				
8 Waterproofed joints	1 Type and method stated		m	M5 Waterproofed joints are only measured where they are specifically required			
9 Guide walls	1 One side 2 Both sides	1 Limitations on design and construction stated	m	M6 The lengths measured for guide walls are those of the diaphragm walls M7 The extent to which excavation, disposal, support, concrete, reinforcement, formwork, and the like are to be included is stated in the item description			
10 Ancillary work in connection with diaphragm walling	1 Preparing cast in pockets or chases at junctions, details stated		item			C2 Preparing cast in pockets or chases is deemed to include removing formwork and preparing cast in reinforcement	
	2 Excavating temporary backfill		m³				
	3 Removal of guide walls	1 One side 2 Both sides	m	M8 The lengths measured for guide walls are those of the diaphragm walls		C3 Removal of guide walls is deemed to include disposal	S5 Limitations on method of disposal
11 Delays	1 Rig standing		h	M9 Delays are only measured where they are specifically authorised		C4 Delays are deemed to include associated labour	

D41 Crib walls/Gabions/Reinforced earth

P1 The following information is shown either on location drawings under A Preliminaries/General conditions or on further drawings which accompany the bills of quantities:

(a) The relative position of crib walls, gabions and earth reinforcement

CLASSIFICATION TABLE

INFORMATION PROVIDED			Unit		MEASUREMENT RULES	DEFINITION RULES	COVERAGE RULES	SUPPLEMENTARY INFORMATION
1 Crib walls	1 Thickness stated	1 Flat undeveloped area	m²	1 Vertical 2 Battering 3 Curved on plan	M1 No deductions are made for openings within crib walls which are part of the modular system, nor for openings ≤ 1.00m²		C1 Crib walls are deemed to include dowels and pins, granular infill and compaction, special units, forming ends and corners, obtaining and providing manufacturer's certificates and for building in pipes and forming small openings	S1 Kind and quality materials
2 Gabion baskets	1 Dimensioned description		Nr.				C2 Gabion baskets are deemed to include assembling, tying and fixing and bracing and tying lids	
3 Filling to gabion baskets (Nr)			m³	1 Selected, details started 2 Treated, details started 3 Specified handling, details started	M2 Filling is measured the nett volume of the basket		C3 Filling is deemed to include compaction and overfilling	
4 Earth reinforcement	1 Fabric	1 Mesh reference	m²	1 Flat 2 Sloping 3 Curved on plan	M3 The area measured for earth reinforcement excludes laps. M4 No deductions are made for voids ≤ 1.00m² in area		C4 Earth reinforcement is deemed to include assembling, tying, fixing, stacking and tensioning	S2 Minimum laps

D50   Underpinning

INFORMATION PROVIDED

P1   The following information is shown either on location drawings under A Preliminaries/General conditions or on further drawings which accompany the bills of quantities:
(a)   the location and extent of the work
(b)   details of the existing structure to be underpinned

P2   Information regarding the nature of excavation work is described in accordance with Section D20 Information Provided

P3   The limit of length carried out in one operation and the number of sections the Contractor is permitted to undertake at one time

CLASSIFICATION TABLE

				MEASUREMENT RULES	DEFINITION RULES	COVERAGE RULES	SUPPLEMENTARY INFORMATION
1 Temporary support for existing structures	1 Particular requirements stated	item					S1 Details of making good
2 Excavating	1 Preliminary trenches 2 Underpinning pits	1 Maximum depth ≤ 0.25 m 2 Maximum depth ≤ 1.00 m 3 Maximum depth ≤ 2.00 m 4 and thereafter in 2.00 m stages	m³	1 Curved 2 From one side only 3 From both sides	M1 Width allowances are related to the total depth of excavation measured from the top of the preliminary trench to the base of the underpinning pit as follows: (a) 1 m where the total depth is ≤ 1.5 m (b) 1.5 m where the total depth is 1.5 – 3m (c) 2 m where the total depth is > 3 m M2 The width of a preliminary trench is calculated as the sum of any projection of the retained foundation beyond the face of the wall plus any projection of the underpinning beyond the face of the retained foundation plus the width allowance M3 The width of an underpinning pit is calculated as the sum of the width of retained foundation plus any projection of the underpinning beyond the face of the retained foundation plus width allowance M4 Items extra over are	D1 Preliminary trenches extend down to the underside of existing foundations D2 Underpinning pits extend from the underside of existing foundations down to the base of the underpinning excavation		
3 Items extra over any type							

				Measurement Rules
				...ith Section D20:7.*.*.*
				M6 Earthwork support to underpinning pits is measured to the back, front and both ends of the underpinning pits and also between each section of the underpinning
5 Cutting away existing projecting foundations	1 Masonry 2 Concrete	1 Maximum width and depth of projection stated	m	
6 Preparing the underside of the existing work to receive the pinning up of the new work	1 Width of existing work stated		m	
7 Disposal				M7 Disposal of water and excavated material are measured in accordance with Section D20:8.*.*.*
8 Filling				M8 Filling is measured in accordance with Section D20:9 & 10.*.*.*
9 Surface treatments				M9 Surface treatments are measured in accordance with Section D20:13.*.*.*
10 Concrete 11 Formwork 12 Reinforcement 13 Brickwork 14 Tanking				M10 Concrete, formwork, reinforcement, brickwork and tanking are measured in accordance with the appropriate Work Sections

E In situ concrete/Large precast concrete

E05 In situ concrete construction generally
E10 Mixing/Casting/Curing in situ concrete

INFORMATION PROVIDED	CLASSIFICATION TABLE			MEASUREMENT RULES	DEFINITION RULES	COVERAGE RULES	SUPPLEMENTARY INFORMATION
P1 The following information is shown either on location drawings or on further drawings under A Preliminaries/General conditions or on further drawings which accompany the bills of quantities: (a) the relative positions of concrete members (b) the size of members (c) the thickness of slabs (d) the permissible loads in relation to casting times				M1 Concrete volume is measured net except that deductions are not made for the following: (a) reinforcement (b) steel sections of area ≤ 0.50 m² (c) cast in accessories (d) voids ≤ 0.05 m³ in volume (except voids in troughed and coffered slabs)		C1 Concrete is deemed to include finishing as struck from basic finish formwork or with a non-mechanical tamped finish unless otherwise required under worked finishes	S1 Kind and quality of materials and mix details S2 Tests of materials and finished work S3 Measures to achieve watertightness S4 Limitations on method, sequence, speed or size of pouring S5 Methods of compaction and curing
	CLASSIFICATION TABLE						S6 Requirement for beds to be laid in bays
	1 Foundations 2 Ground beams 3 Isolated foundations		m³		D1 Foundations include attached column bases and attached pile caps D2 Isolated foundations include isolated column bases, isolated pile caps and machine bases		
	4 Beds 5 Slabs 6 Coffered and troughed slabs 7 Walls 8 Filling hollow walls	1 Reinforced 2 Reinforced > 5% 3 Sloping ≤ 15° 4 Sloping > 15° 5 Poured on or against earth or unblinded hardcore	1 Thickness ≤ 150 mm 2 Thickness 150 – 450 mm 3 Thickness > 450 mm	M2 The thickness range stated in descriptions excludes projections and recesses M3 The thickness range stated of coffered and troughed slabs is measured overall	D3 Beds include: (a) blinding beds (b) plinths (c) thickenings of beds D4 Slabs include: (a) attached beams and beam casings whose depth is ≤ three times their width (depth measured below the slab) (b) column drop heads D5 Coffered and troughed slabs include margins whose width is ≤ 500mm. Wider margins are included with ordinary slabs D6 Walls include attached		
	9 Beams 10 Beam casings	1 Reinforced 2 Reinforced > 5%	1 Isolated 2 Isolated deep 3 Attached deep				

		Unit	Measurement rules	Definition rules
13 Staircases			depth (measured below the slab where attached) is > three times their width	D8 Staircases include landings and strings
14 Upstands				D9 Upstands exclude kickers
15 Items extra over the in situ concrete in which they occur	1 Working around heating panels	m²	isolated and when their length on plan is ≤ four times their thickness	

	2 Monolithic finishes, thickness stated
	  1 Top surface sloping ≤ 15°
	  2 Top surface sloping > 15°
			M5 The area measured is the system area	D10 Monolithic finishes include those which are cast onto concrete by lining formwork

16 Grouting	1 Stanchion bases 2 Grillages	nr		
17 Filling	1 Mortices	nr		
	2 Holes, (nr)	m³		
	3 Chases > 0.01 m²	m³		
	4 Chases ≤ 0.01 m²	m		

E11 Sprayed in situ concrete

INFORMATION PROVIDED	MEASUREMENT RULES	DEFINITION RULES	COVERAGE RULES	SUPPLEMENTARY INFORMATION
P1 The following information is shown either on location drawings under A Preliminaries/General conditions or on further drawings which accompany the bills of quantities: (a) the relative positions of sprayed concrete members (b) the permissible loads in relation to casting times				

CLASSIFICATION TABLE

					MEASUREMENT RULES	DEFINITION RULES	COVERAGE RULES	SUPPLEMENTARY INFORMATION
1 Slabs	1 Thickness stated	1 Tops 2 Soffits	m²	1 Curved	M1 Reinforcement is measured in Section E30			S1 Kind and quality of materials S2 Preparatory work S3 Method of application and finish
2 Walls								
3 Beams								
4 Columns								

E20 Formwork for in situ concrete

INFORMATION PROVIDED

P1 The following information is shown either on location drawings under A Preliminaries/General conditions or on further drawings which accompany the bills of quantities:
- (a) the relative positions of concrete members
- (b) the size of members
- (c) the thickness of slabs
- (d) the permissible loads in relation to casting times

CLASSIFICATION TABLE				MEASUREMENT RULES	DEFINITION RULES	COVERAGE RULES	SUPPLEMENTARY INFORMATION
				M1 Except where otherwise stated, formwork is measured to concrete surfaces of the finished structure which require temporary support during casting	D1 Plain formwork surfaces are those which contain no steps, rebates, pockets or other discontinuities	C1 Formwork is deemed to include adaptation to accommodate projecting pipes, reinforcing bars and the like	S1 Kind and quality of materials and propping requirements for permanent formwork
				M2 Curved work is so described with the radii stated	D2 Formwork left in is that which is not designed to remain in position but is nonetheless impossible to remove	C2 Formwork is deemed to include all cutting, splayed edges and the like	S2 Basic finish where not at the discretion of the Contractor
					D3 Permanent formwork is that which is designed to remain in position		
1 Sides of foundations	1 Plain vertical	m²	1 Left in	M3 Passings of ground beams are not deducted from area of formwork	D4 Foundations include bases and pile caps		
2 Sides of ground beams and edges of beds	2 Dimensioned description	m	2 Permanent		D5 Edges of suspended slabs exclude those associated with attached beams at slab perimeters		
3 Edges of suspended slabs	2 Height ≤ 250 mm						
4 Sides of upstands	3 Height 250 – 500 mm						
5 Steps in top surfaces	4 Height 500 mm – 1.00 m						
6 Steps in soffits	1 Height > 1.00 m						
7 Machine bases and plinths							
8 Soffits of slabs	1 Slab thickness ≤ 200 mm	m²	1 Height to soffit ≤ 1.50 m	M4 Voids ≤ 5.00 m² irrespective of location are not deducted from the area measured	D6 Formwork to soffits of slabs includes formwork to landings occurring at floor levels		
9 Soffits of landings (nr)	2 and thereafter in 100 mm stages		2 and thereafter in 1.50 m stages	M5 Soffits of coffered or troughed slabs are measured as if to a plain surface			
			3 Left in	M6 The thickness stated of the coffered or troughed slabs is measured overall			
			4 Permanent				
10 Soffits of coffered or troughed slabs	1 Size of mould and profile, centres of mould, and slab thickness stated				D7 Soffits of coffered or troughed slabs include margins which are ≤ 500 mm wide		
11 Top formwork			1 Left in	M7 Top formwork is measured for surfaces sloping > 15° or where otherwise specifically required			
	1 Horizontal		2 Permanent				
	2 Sloping ≤ 15°						
	3 Sloping > 15°						

E20 continued

CLASSIFICATION TABLE				MEASUREMENT RULES	DEFINITION RULES	COVERAGE RULES	SUPPLEMENTARY INFORMATION
12 Walls		1 Vertical 2 Battered	m²	1 Height > 3.00 m above floor level 2 Interrupted 3 To one side only, wall thickness and background to other side stated 4 Left in 5 Permanent to both sides 6 Permanent to one side only, wall thickness and background to other side stated	M8 Voids ≤ 5.00 m² irrespective of location are not deducted from the area measured for walls M9 The area measured for walls whose height is > 3.00 m includes the area below 3.00 m high M10 The area of wall kickers is not deducted	D8 Walls include isolated columns and column casings whose length on plan is > four times their thickness	
13 Beams (nr) 14 Beam casings (nr)	1 Attached to slabs 2 Attached to walls 3 Isolated	1 Regular shaped, shape stated	m²	1 Height to soffit ≤ 1.50 m 2 and thereafter in 1.50 m stages	M11 Passings of subsidiary beams or other projections are not deducted from areas of formwork but such intersections are deemed to constitute the commencement of an additional member	D9 Where a downstand beam is formed by temporary formwork but the slab is supported by permanent formwork the downstand beam is regarded as an isolated beam	C3 Formwork to beams, columns and column casings is deemed to include ends
		2 Irregular shaped, dimensioned diagram	m	3 Left in 4 Permanent				
15 Columns (nr) 16 Column casings (nr)	1 Attached to walls 2. Isolated			1 Height > 3.00 m above floor level 2 Left in 3 Permanent	M12 Formwork to edges of suspended slabs associated with attached beams at slab perimeters is included with the measurement of the formwork to such beams M13 Recesses, nibs or rebates which occur in beam or column formwork measured in accordance with 13 – 16. * . 2. * are included in the measurement of such formwork	D10 Regular shaped includes rectangular, circular, hexagonal or other definable regular shape	
17 Recesses (nr) 18 Nibs (nr) 19 Rebates (nr)	1 Dimensioned description		m	1 Extra over the formwork in which they occur 2 Left in 3 Permanent	M14 Recesses, nibs and rebates are only measured as extra over on superficial items of formwork		C4 Formwork to recesses is deemed to include ends
20 Extra over a basic finish for formed finishes	1 Slabs 2 Walls 3 Beams 4 Columns		m²			D11 Formed finishes are those where a finish other than a basic finish is required		S3 Details of formed finishes

	First division	Second division	Third division	Supplementary information	Measurement rules / Definition rules
22 Suspended wall kickers					
23 Wall ends, soffits and steps in walls	1 Plain	m²			the centre line of the wall and is deemed to include both sides
	2 Dimensioned description				
24 Openings in walls		2 Width ≤ 250 mm	m	2 Permanent	
		3 Width 250 – 500 mm			
		4 Width 500 mm – 1.00 m			
		1 Width > 1.00 m			
25 Stairflights (nr)	1 Width of stairflight stated, waist and risers described	1 String, width stated	m	1 Left in	M16 Lengths of stairflights are measured between top and bottom nosings
		2 String, dimensioned diagram		2 Permanent	M17 Widths are measured overall
	2 Dimensioned diagram			3 Junction with wall	C5 Formwork to stairflights is deemed to include soffits, risers and strings
26 Mortices	1 Girth ≤ 500 mm	1 Depth ≤ 250 mm	nr	1 Rectangular	D12 Mortices include pockets
27 Holes	2 Girth 500 mm – 1.00 m	2 Depth 250 – 500 mm		2 Circular	D13 Holes are those ≤ 5.00 m²
	3 and thereafter in 1.00 m stages	3 Depth 500 mm – 1.00 m		3 Irregular shape, dimensioned description	
		4 Depth > 1.00 m depth stated		4 Left in	
				5 Permanent	
28 Complex shapes	1 Dimensioned description		nr	1 Left in	
	2 Dimensioned diagram			2 Permanent	

E30 Reinforcement for in situ concrete

INFORMATION PROVIDED				MEASUREMENT RULES	DEFINITION RULES	COVERAGE RULES	SUPPLEMENTARY INFORMATION
P1 The following information is shown either on location drawings under A Preliminaries/General conditions or on further drawings which accompany the bills of quantities: (a) the relative positions of concrete members (b) the size of members (c) the thickness of slabs (d) the permissible loads in relation to casting times							S1 Kind and quality of materials S2 Details of tests S3 Bending restrictions

CLASSIFICATION TABLE

				MEASUREMENT RULES	DEFINITION RULES	COVERAGE RULES	SUPPLEMENTARY INFORMATION
1 Bar	1 Nominal size stated	1 Straight 2 Bent 3 Curved	t	M1 The weight of bar reinforcement excludes surface treatments and rolling margin M2 The stage lengths in the fourth column are the lengths before bending	D1 Horizontal bars include bars sloping ≤ 30° from horizontal D2 Vertical bars include bars sloping > 30° from horizontal	C1 Bar reinforcement is deemed to include hooks and tying wire, and spacers and chairs which are at the discretion of the Contractor	
		1 Horizontal, length 12.00 – 15.00 m 2 and thereafter in 3.00 m stages 3 Vertical, length 6.00 – 9.00 m 4 and thereafter in 3.00 m stages					
		4 Links					
2 Spacers and chairs	1 Dimensioned description		t	M3 Spacers, chairs and special joints are measured only where they are not at the discretion of the Contractor			
3 Special joint	2 Nominal size and type stated		nr				
4 Fabric	1 Mesh reference and weight per m² stated	1 Bent 2 Strips in one width, width stated	m²	M4 The area measured for fabric excludes laps. M5 Voids ≤ 1.00 m² in area are not deducted		C2 Fabric reinforcement is deemed to include laps, tying wire, all cutting and bending, and spacers and chairs which are at the discretion of the Contractor C3 Bent fabric reinforcement is deemed to include that wrapped around steel members	S4 Minimum laps

SUPPLEMENTARY INFORMATION

P1 The following information is shown either on location drawings under A Preliminaries/General conditions or on further drawings which accompany the bills of quantities:
(a) the relative positions of concrete members
(b) the size of members
(c) the thickness of slabs
(d) the permissible loads in relation to casting times

CLASSIFICATION TABLE

				MEASUREMENT RULES	DEFINITION RULES	COVERAGE RULES	SUPPLEMENTARY INFORMATION
1 Members tensioned (nr)	1 Dimensioned description	nr	1 Composite construction	M1 Post tensioning is measured by the number of tendons in identical members			S1 Number, length, material and size of wires in tendons S2 Ducts, vents and grouting S3 Anchorages and end treatment S4 Stressing sequence, transfer stress, initial stress S5 Limitation on propping

E40 Designed joints in in situ concrete

INFORMATION PROVIDED					MEASUREMENT RULES	DEFINITION RULES	COVERAGE RULES	SUPPLEMENTARY INFORMATION
P1 Information is shown on location drawings under A Preliminaries/General conditions					M1 Construction joints located at the discretion of the Contractor are not measured			S1 Kind and quality of materials

CLASSIFICATION TABLE

					MEASUREMENT RULES	DEFINITION RULES	COVERAGE RULES	SUPPLEMENTARY INFORMATION
1 Plain 2 Formed 3 Cut	1 Width or depth ≤ 150 mm 2 and thereafter in 150 mm stages	m	1 Dimensioned description	1 Curved	M2 The width or depth of joints is measured overall	D1 Plain joints are those which do not require formwork	C1 Formed joints are deemed to include formwork	S2 Details of fillers, waterstops, dowels, backing strips and reinforcement crossing joints
4 Sealants							C2 Work is deemed to include preparation, cleaners, primers and sealers	S3 Method of application S4 Preparation of contact surfaces, cleaners, primers and sealers
5 Angles in waterstops 6 Intersections in waterstops		nr			M3 Angles and intersections are measured only where they are welded or purpose made			

E41 Worked finishes/Cutting to in situ concrete

INFORMATION PROVIDED			MEASUREMENT RULES	DEFINITION RULES	COVERAGE RULES	SUPPLEMENTARY INFORMATION
P1 Information is shown on location drawings under A Preliminaries/General conditions			M1 Curved work is so described			
CLASSIFICATION TABLE						S1 Description of finish required and method of achieving where not at the discretion of the Contractor
1 Tamping by mechanical means 2 Power floating 3 Trowelling 4 Hacking 5 Grinding 6 Sandblasting 7 Finishings achieved by other means	m²	1 Sloping 2 Falls 3 Crossfalls 4 Soffits				
8 Cutting chases 9 Cutting rebates	m	1 Specific width stated 2 Making good 3 In reinforced concrete	1 Depth ≤ 50 mm 2 Depth 50 – 100 mm 3 Depth 100 – 150 mm 4 Depth > 150 mm, depth stated	M2 Width is required to be stated only where there is a specific width requirement		
10 Cutting mortices 11 Cutting holes	nr	1 Specific cross sectional size stated 2 Making good 3 In reinforced concrete	1 Depth ≤ 100 mm 2 Depth 100 – 200 mm 3 Depth 200 – 300 mm 4 Depth > 300 mm, depth stated	M3 Cross sectional size is required to be stated only where there is a specific cross sectional size requirement		

P1 The following information is shown either on location drawings under A Preliminaries/General conditions or on further drawings which accompany the bills of quantities:
(a) the relative positions of concrete members
(b) the size of members
(c) the thickness of slabs
(d) the permissible loads in relation to casting times

CLASSIFICATION TABLE

1 Type or name stated	1 Dimensioned description	m²	m	nr	1 Spacing dimensions stated	M1 Cast-in accessories are normally measured by number (nr). Linear or area measure may be used provided that any appropriate spacing dimensions are given in descriptions	D1 Cast-in accessories include anchor bolts, anchor boxes, anchor fixing bolts etc., dowels, column guards and isolated glass lenses. Cast-in accessories exclude reinforcement, tying wire, distance blocks, spacers, chairs, structural steelwork, hollow blocks, filler blocks, permanent formwork, joints and all components around which concrete is cast, but which are not fixed by the Contractor	S1 Kind and quality of materials and sizes or manufacturer's reference

E50 **Precast concrete frame structures**
F31 **Precast concrete sills/lintels/copings/features**
H40 **Glassfibre reinforced cement panel cladding/features**
H42 **Precast concrete panel cladding/features**
H50 **Precast concrete slab cladding/features**
K33 **Concrete/Terrazzo partitions**

53

INFORMATION PROVIDED		MEASUREMENT RULES	DEFINITION RULES	COVERAGE RULES	SUPPLEMENTARY INFORMATION
P1 The following information is either shown on location drawings under A Preliminaries/General conditions or on further drawings which accompany the bills of quantities: (a) details of precast concrete members showing stressing arrangements (b) full details of anchorages, ducts, sheathing and vents (c) the relative positions of concrete members (d) the size of members (e) the thickness of slabs (f) the permissible loads					

CLASSIFICATION TABLE

		Unit		MEASUREMENT RULES	COVERAGE RULES	SUPPLEMENTARY INFORMATION
1 Type or name stated	1 Dimensioned description	nr		M1 Precast units are normally measured by number (nr). Linear measurement may be used where the length of units is at the discretion of the Contractor, where the individual units are of an identical standard length, or where otherwise identical units vary in their length. In these cases the number of units is stated	C1 Precast units are deemed to include moulds, reinforcement, bedding, fixings, temporary supports, cast-in accessories and pretensioning	S1 Kind and quality of materials and mix details S2 Tests of materials and finished work S3 Methods of compaction and curing S4 Bedding and fixing S5 Surface finishes S6 Kind and quality of pretensioning materials, spacing and stresses
	2 Dimensioned description	m (nr)	1 Reinforcement, details stated 2 Cast-in accessories, details stated			
	3 Dimensioned description 1 Floor units, length stated	m²		M2 Where floor units are of the same length they may be measured in square metres and grouped together stating length		
2 Items extra over the units on which they occur	1 Angles 2 Fair ends 3 Stoolings 4 Others, details stated	nr		M3 Where units are measured linear, angles, fair ends, stoolings and the like are enumerated as extra over the units		
3 Joints	1 Dimensioned profile description 1 Sizes of filling and sealants stated	m		M4 Enumerated joints may be given in the description of the precast items in which...		S7 Kind and quality of materials

P1 The following information is shown either on location drawings under A Preliminaries/General conditions or on further drawings which accompany the bill of quantities:
- (a) details of purpose-made, prestressed concrete members showing stressing arrangements
- (b) full details of anchorages, ducts, sheathing and vents
- (c) the relative positions of concrete members
- (d) the size of members
- (e) the thickness of slabs
- (f) the permissible loads

CLASSIFICATION TABLE

				MEASUREMENT RULES	DEFINITION RULES	COVERAGE RULES	INFORMATION
1 Composite slabs	1 Thickness stated	m²	1 Sloping ≤ 15° 2 Sloping > 15°	M1 The thickness stated for composite slabs is measured overall M2 Composite slabs are measured over margins ≤ 500 mm wide M3 Margins > 500 mm wide are measured as ordinary slabs in Sections E10, E20 and E30	D1 Composite slabs include margins ≤ 500 mm wide, wider margins are included with ordinary slabs	C1 Composite slabs are deemed to include solid concrete work and filling ends	S1 Kind and quality of materials, sizes and spacings of planks and blocks S2 Top finish S3 Soffit finish S4 Margins S5 Formwork S6 Reinforcement and prestressing arrangements
2 Formwork				M4 Formwork to in situ component of work is measured in accordance with Section E20			
3 Reinforcement				M5 Reinforcement to in situ component of work is measured in accordance with Section E30			

F Masonry

F10 Brick/Block walling
F11 Glass block walling

INFORMATION PROVIDED	MEASUREMENT RULES	DEFINITION RULES	COVERAGE RULES	SUPPLEMENTARY INFORMATION
P1 The following information is shown either on location drawings under A Preliminaries/General conditions or on further drawings of which accompany the bills of quantities: (a) Plans of each floor level and principal sections showing the position of and the materials used in the walls (b) External elevations showing the materials used	M1 Brickwork and blockwork unless otherwise stated are measured on the centre line of the material M2 No deductions are made for the following: (a) voids ≤ 0.10 m² (b) flues, lined flues and flue blocks where voids and work displaced are together ≤ 0.25 m² M3 Deductions for string courses, lintels, sills, plates and the like are measured as regards height to the extent only of full brick or block courses displaced and as regards depth to the extent only of full half brick beds displaced M4 Curved work is so described with the radii stated	D1 Thickness stated is nominal thickness unless defined otherwise below D2 Facework is any work in bricks or blocks finished fair D3 Work is deemed vertical unless otherwise described D4 Walls include skins of hollow walls	C1 Brickwork and blockwork are deemed to include: (a) extra materials for curved work (b) all rough and fair cutting (c) forming rough and fair grooves, throats, mortices, chases, rebates and holes, stops and mitres (d) raking out joints to form a key (e) labours in eaves filling (f) labours in returns, ends and angles (g) centering	S1 Kind, quality and size of bricks or blocks S2 Type of bond S3 Composition and mix of mortar S4 Type of pointing S5 Method of cutting where not at the discretion of the Contractor

CLASSIFICATION TABLE

1 Walls 2 Isolated piers 3 Isolated casings 4 Chimney stacks	1 Thickness stated 2 Facework one side, thickness stated 3 Facework both sides, thickness stated	1 Vertical 2 Battering 3 Tapering, one side 4 Tapering, both sides	m²	1 Building against other work 2 Bonding to other work 3 Used as formwork, details of temporary strutting stated 4 Building overhand	M5 Building against other work and bonding is measured where the other work is existing or consists of a differing material	D5 Battering walls are sloping walls with parallel sides D6 Tapering walls are walls of diminishing thickness D7 Thickness stated for tapering walls is mean thickness D8 Isolated piers are isolated walls whose length on plan is ≤ four times their thickness, except where	C2 Brickwork and blockwork bonded to another material is deemed to include extra material for bonding

	First classification	Second classification	Unit	Supplementary information	Measurement rules	Definition and Coverage rules	Supplementary rules
(continued)		3 Horizontal	m	1 Building from outside scaffolding		thickness), plinths, oversailing courses and the like	
6 Arches (nr)	1 Height on face, thickness and width of exposed soffit and shape of arch stated				M6 Arches are measured the mean girth or length on face		
7 Isolated chimney shafts and the like (nr)	1 Size on plan, shape and overall height stated						
8 Boiler seatings	1 Thickness stated		m²				
9 Flue linings	1 Thickness stated		m²		M7 Non brick masonry flue linings are measured in Section F30:11.1.0.0		
10 Boiler seating kerbs	1 Shape and size stated		m				
11 Items extra over the work in which they occur	1 Specials, dimensioned description	1 Reveals 2 Angles 3 Intersections	m				
12 Closing cavities	1 Width of cavity and method of closing stated	1 Vertical 2 Raking 3 Horizontal	m				
13 Facework ornamental bands and the like, type stated	1 Flush 2 Sunk, depth of set back stated 3 Projecting, depth of set forward stated	1 Vertical, width stated 2 Raking, width stated 3 Horizontal, width stated 4 Others, details stated	m	1 Extra over the work in which they occur 2 Entirely of stretchers 3 Entirely of headers 4 Building overhand		D10 Radii stated are mean radii on face D11 Facework ornamental bands and the like are brick-on-edge bands, brick-on-end bands, basket pattern bands, moulded or splayed plinth cappings, moulded string courses, moulded cornices and the like	
14 Facework quoins	1 Flush 2 Sunk, depth of set back stated 3 Projecting, depth of set forward stated	1 Mean girth stated	m	1 Extra over the work in which they occur 2 Cut and rubbed 3 Rusticated 4 Tile inserts included 5 Building overhand	M8 Facework quoins are measured on the vertical angle	D12 Facework quoins are formed with facing bricks which differ in kind or size from the general facings	S6 Method of jointing quoins to brick or blockwork

CLASSIFICATION TABLE			MEASUREMENT RULES	DEFINITION RULES	COVERAGE RULES	SUPPLEMENTARY INFORMATION
15 Facework sills 16 Facework thresholds 17 Facework copings 18 Facework steps	1 Dimensioned description	m	1 Vertical 2 Raking 3 Horizontal 4 Others, details stated			S7 Method of forming sills, thresholds, copings and steps
19 Facework tumblings to buttresses 20 Facework key blocks 21 Facework corbels 22 Facework bases to pilasters 23 Facework cappings to pilasters 24 Facework cappings to isolated piers		nr	1 Extra over the work in which they occur			
25 Bonding to existing	1 Thickness of new work stated	m				
26 Surface treatments	1 Type and purpose stated	m²	1 Extra over the work in which they occur 2 Building overhand 3 Set weathering	D13 This item does not include application of materials to the wall		

F20 Natural stone rubble walling
F21 Natural stone ashlar walling/dressings
F22 Cast stone ashlar walling/dressings

INFORMATION PROVIDED	MEASUREMENT RULES	DEFINITION RULES	COVERAGE RULES	SUPPLEMENTARY INFORMATION
P1 The following information is shown either on location drawings under A Preliminaries/General conditions or on further drawings which accompany the bills of quantities: (a) plans of each floor level and principal sections showing the position of and the materials used in the walls (b) external elevations showing the materials used	M1 Stonework is measured according to mean dimensions M2 No deduction is made for: (a) voids ≤ 0.10 m² (b) flues, lined flues and flue blocks where voids and work displaced are together ≤ 0.25 m² M3 Linear and enumerated items shall identify grooves, throats, flutes, rebates, cutting and mortices M4 Curved work is so described with the radii stated	D1 The thickness stated is the nominal thickness except where defined otherwise below D2 Stone dressings are those in walls of other materials D3 Dimensioned diagrams are given unless a written description is sufficient for full clarity D4 Work is deemed vertical unless otherwise described	C1 The work is deemed to include: (a) extra stone for joints (b) extra materials for curved work (c) mortices, (other than linear items) holes, stops and arrises (d) raking out joints to form key (e) metal cramps, slate dowels, metal dowels, lead plugs and the like (f) labours in eaves filling (g) labours in returns, ends and angles (h) dressed margins to rubble work (j) levelling uncoursed work (k) templets and patterns (l) rough and fair square cutting	S1 Kind and quality of materials and, for rubble walling, whether of random or squared stones, built with or without mortar and where coursed the average height of the courses or maximum and minimum heights of diminishing course S2 Coatings to backs of stones S3 Coatings to surface of finished work S4 Cleaning on completion S5 Composition and mix of mortar S6 Type of pointing S7 Method of jointing together and fixing S8 Thickness, mix and colour of the facing material to cast stonework S9 Stones not set on their natural bed S10 Type and positioning of metal cramps, slates, dowels, metal dowels, lead plugs and the like

F20/F21/F22 continued

CLASSIFICATION TABLE		Unit		MEASUREMENT RULES	DEFINITION RULES	COVERAGE RULES	SUPPLEMENTARY INFORMATION
1 Walls 2 Chimney stacks	1 Thickness stated	m²	1 Vertical 2 Battering 3 Tapering, one side 4 Tapering, both sides	M5 Building against other work and bonding to other work is measured where the other work is existing or consists of a differing material	D5 Battering walls are sloping walls with parallel sides D6 Tapering walls are walls of diminishing thickness D7 Thickness stated for tapering walls is mean thickness D8 Walls include skins of hollow walls	C2 Battering and tapering walls are deemed to include the extra materials required C3 Work is deemed to include extra material for bonding	S11 Method of bonding to backing S12 Type and spacing of fixing and method of securing to backing
			1 Blocks > 1.50 m long 2 Blocks > 0.50 m³ 3 Stone dressings 4 Faced one side 5 Faced both sides 6 Building against other work 7 Building against other battered work				
3 Isolated columns 4 Attached columns	1 Dimensioned description	m	8 Bonding to other work 9 Sunk to entasis, greatest size stated 10 Plain 11 Sunk 12 Circular 13 Circular-circular 14 Rusticated or fluted 15 Used as formwork, details of temporary strutting stated		D9 Columns are walls whose length on plan is ≤ four times their thickness, except where caused by openings D10 Attached columns include attached piers and pilasters D11 The dimensioned description stated for attached columns refers to the projection only		
5 Vaulting	1 Thickness and type stated	m²	16 With stoolings (nr)				
6 Lintels 7 Sills 8 Mullions 9 Transoms	1 Dimensioned description ‐ ‐ ‐ ‐ ‐ ‐ ‐ ‐ ‐ ‐ 2 Dimensioned diagram	m	17 Band courses with returned ends (nr) 18 Building overhand				
10 Quoin stones 11 Jamb stones	1 Dimensioned description 1 Attached 2 Attached with different finish, type of finish stated 3 Isolated	m		M6 Quoins and jambs are measured on the vertical angle	D12 Attached stones are those attached to the same type of stone walling D13 Isolated stones are those attached to another form of construction		
12 Slab architraves 13 Slab surrounds to openings	1 Dimensioned description	m			D14 Slabs are those which are not bonded to their surrounding work		

			Unit	Supplementary information
				and attached piers. Mouldings are given in the description of linear items
(...rse courses)				the like
16 Copings	3 Horizontal			D16 Plain bands > 300 mm wide are measured as walling or facework
17 Handrails	4 Others, details stated			
18 Cappings				
19 Kerbs				
20 Cover stones				
21 Steps (nr)	1 Plain		m	D17 Spandrel steps are steps with sloping soffits
	2 Spandrel			
22 Winders	1 Stones (nr)		nr	
23 Landings				
24 Arches (nr)	1 Height of face, width of soffit and shape of arch stated		m	M8 Arches are measured the mean girth or length on face
			nr	M9 The quantity (nr) is only stated in an item which is measured linearly
25 Closing cavities	1 Width of cavity and method of closing stated	1 Vertical	m	
		2 Raking		
		3 Horizontal		
26 Rough raking or circular cutting	1 Thickness stated		m	
27 Fair raking or circular cutting				
28 Grooves	1 Size stated		m	M10 Grooves, throats, flutes, and rebates are only measured separately on superficial items of masonry and attached piers
29 Throats				
30 Flutes				
31 Rebates				
32 Chases	1 Rough	1 Girth ≤ 150 mm	m	
	2 Fair	2 and thereafter in 150 mm stages		

F20/F21/F22 continued

CLASSIFICATION TABLE				MEASUREMENT RULES	DEFINITION RULES	COVERAGE RULES	SUPPLEMENTARY INFORMATION
33 Special purpose stones	1 Function stated	nr	1 Plain cuboid, dimensions stated 2 Dimensioned description	M11 Descriptions of stones are given as the smallest block from which each item can be obtained having regard in the case of natural stone to the plane in which the stone is required to be laid with relation to its quarry bed. The dimensions are taken over one mortar bed and one mortar joint			
34 Carvings 35 Sculptures	1 Character of work stated	nr	1 Component drawing			C4 Carvings and sculptures are deemed to include: (a) selecting blocks of stone for size and quality (b) boasting for carving (c) working mouldings or similar members	
			1 Providing models				
36 Centering	1 Arches 2 Tracery 3 Projecting masonry 4 Vaulting	nr	1 Dimensioned description	M12 A dimensioned description of centering gives the shape and width of the surface to be supported, the span of the soffit, and, in the case of arches, whether segmental, semicircular, invert and the like, stating the rise		C5 Centering is deemed to include: (a) strutting, shoring, bolting, wedging, easing, striking and removing (b) cutting (c) scribed and splayed edges (d) notching for key blocks, projecting voussiors and the like	S13 Nature of supported surface
			1 Sloping soffits 2 Maximum support height 3.00 – 4.50 m 3 and thereafter in 1.50 m stages 4 Left in				

INFORMATION PROVIDED

P1 The following information is shown either on location drawings under A Preliminaries/General conditions or on further drawings which accompany the bills of quantities:
(a) plans of each floor level and principal sections showing the position of and the materials used in the walls
(b) external elevations showing the materials used

CLASSIFICATION TABLE

Item			Unit		MEASUREMENT RULES	DEFINITION RULES	COVERAGE RULES	SUPPLEMENTARY INFORMATION
					M1 Curved work is so described		C1 Accessories are deemed to include: (a) rough and fair cutting on walls around accessories (b) bedding and pointing accessories (c) extra materials for curved work	S1 Kind and quality of materials
1 Forming cavities	1 In hollow walls 2 Between walls and other work	1 Width of cavity stated 1 Rigid sheet cavity insulation, thickness stated	m²					S2 Type, size and spacing of wall ties S3 Type, thickness and method of fixing cavity insulation
2 Damp proof courses	1 Width ≤ 225 mm 2 Width > 225 mm	1 Vertical 2 Raking 3 Horizontal 4 Stepped 1 Cavity trays	m²		M2 No allowance is made for laps M3 No deduction is made for voids ≤ 0.50 m²		C2 Damp proof courses are deemed to include pointing exposed edges	S4 Gauge, thickness or substance of sheet materials S5 Number of layers S6 Composition and mix of bedding materials
3 Joint reinforcement	1 Width stated		m		M4 No allowance is made for laps			S7 Minimum laps
4 Weather fillets 5 Angle fillets	1 Size stated		m				C3 Fillets are deemed to include ends and angles	
6 Pointing in flashings			m		M5 Flashings are measured in Sections H70–H76		C4 Pointing in flashings is deemed to include cutting or forming grooves or chases	
7 Wedging and pinning	1 Width of wall stated		m					
8 Joints	1 Dimensioned description		m		M6 Joints are only measured where designed		C5 Work is deemed to include preparation, cleaners, primers and sealers	S8 Type of filler and sealant S9 Method of application S10 Preparation of contact surfaces, cleaners, primers and sealers
9 Slates and tiles for creasing 10 Slate and tile sills	1 Width stated	1 Courses (nr)	m				C6 Slates and tiles for creasing and sills are deemed to include ends, angles and pointing	

F30 continued

CLASSIFICATION TABLE			MEASUREMENT RULES	DEFINITION RULES	COVERAGE RULES	SUPPLEMENTARY INFORMATION
11 Flue linings	1 Dimensioned description	m	M7 Brick flue linings are measured in Section F10:9.1.0.0		C7 Flue linings are deemed to include: (a) cutting to form easings (b) cutting to form bends (c) cutting to walls around linings	S11 Method of building
12 Air bricks 13 Ventilating gratings 14 Soot doors	1 Size of opening, nature and thickness of wall stated	nr 1 Lintels, details stated 2 Arches, details stated			C8 Air bricks, ventilating gratings, soot doors and the like are deemed to include any necessary forming of openings, liners, cavity closers and damp proof courses	
15 Gas flue blocks	1 Size of block and number of flues in each stated	nr				S12 Method of building
16 Proprietary items	1 Dimensioned description 1 Manufacturer's reference	nr				S13 Method of fixing

G Structural/Carcassing metal/timber

G10 Structural steel framing
G11 Structural aluminium framing
G12 Isolated structural metal members

INFORMATION PROVIDED

P1 The following information is shown either on location drawngs under A Preliminaries/General conditions or on further drawings which accompany the bills of quantities:
(a) the position of the work in relation to other parts of the work and of the proposed buildings
(b) the types and sizes of structural members and their positions in relation to each other
(c) details of connections or of the reactions, moments and axial loads at connection points

CLASSIFICATION TABLE

Classification				MEASUREMENT RULES	DEFINITION RULES	COVERAGE RULES	SUPPLEMENTARY INFORMATION
1 Framing, fabrication	1 Columns 2 Beams 3 Bracings	1 Castellated 2 Tapered 3 Curved 4 Cambered 5 Hollow, shape stated	t	M1 The mass of framing includes all components except fittings M2 Fittings are all grouped together irrespective of the member to which they are attached M3 The mass of framing is measured from their overall lengths with no deductions for splay cuts or mitred ends or for the mass of metal removed to form notches and holes each < 0.10 m² in area measured in the plane M4 No allowance is made for the mass of weld fillets, black bolts, nuts, washers, rivets and protective coatings M5 The mass of steel is taken for measurement as 785 kg/m² per 100 mm	D1 Fabrication includes all operations up to and including delivery to site D2 Purlins and cladding rails are measured by weight when hot rolled D3 Wires, cables, rods and bars include sag rods, ties and the like D4 Special bolts and fasteners are those other than black bolts and holding down bolts or assemblies	C1 Items for fabrication measured by weight are deemed to include shop and site black bolts, nuts and washers for structural framing to structural framing connections	S1 Types and grades of materials S2 Details of welding tests and X-rays S3 Details of performance tests
	4 Purlins and cladding rails 5 Grillages						
	6 Overhead crane rails	1 Details of fixing clips and resilient pads stated					
	7 Trestles, towers and built up columns 8 Trusses and built up girders	1 Details of construction stated					
	9 Wires, cables, rods and bars 10 Fittings						
	11 Holding down bolts or assemblies	1 Details stated	nr				
	12 Special bolts and fasteners	1 Type and diameter stated					

	site				fabrication		
3 Permanent formwork	1 Type and method of fixing stated	1 Curved	m²			D6 Permanent formwork is that which is structurally integral with the framing	
4 Cold rolled purlins and cladding rails	1 Type and method of fixing stated		m				
5 Isolated structural member	1 Plain member use stated 2 Built-up member use and details of construction stated	1 Weight ≤40 kg/m 2 Weight 40–100 kg/m 3 Weight >100 kg/m	t	1 Castellated 2 Tapered 3 Curved 4 Cambered 5 Hollow, shape stated	M6 The mass of built up members is calculated as defined from 'Framing, fabrication' M7 Fixing bolts are measured in accordance with the rules contained in Section G20:25.*.0.0	D7 An isolated structural member is a member not part of a framing as measured under 1.1 – 12 D8 Use is defined as 1.1 – 1.9 inclusive D9 Fixing bolts are bolts fixing an isolated structural member to another element	C2 Isolated structural members are deemed to include fabrication and erection
	3 Fittings	1 Details stated					
6 Filling hollow sections	1 Water 2 Concrete		item				
7 Surface preparation	1 Blast cleaning 2 Pickling 3 Wire brushing 4 Flame cleaning 5 Others, details stated		m²				S4 Type of preparation, details of application and timing
8 Surface treatment	1 Galvanising 2 Sprayed metal coating 3 Protective painting 4 Others, details stated		m²				
9 Localised protective coating	1 Type stated		m²		M8 Localised protective coating is only measured to structural aluminium framing	D10 Localised protective coatings are localised applications to surfaces in contact with dissimilar metals and aggressive building materials	

G20 Carpentry/Timber framing/First fixing

INFORMATION PROVIDED			MEASUREMENT RULES	DEFINITION RULES	COVERAGE RULES	SUPPLEMENTARY INFORMATION
P1 The following information is shown either on location drawings under A Preliminaries/General conditions or on further drawings which accompany the bills of quantities: (a) the scope and location of the work				D1 All sizes are nominal sizes unless stated as finished sizes	C1 The work is deemed to include labours on items of timber, except as otherwise required	S1 Kind and quality of materials and if timber whether sawn or wrot S2 Method of fixing where not at the discretion of the Contractor S3 Fixing through vulnerable materials S4 Preservative treatments applied as part of the production process S5 Surface treatments applied as part of the production process S6 Selection and protection for subsequent treatment S7 Matching grain or colour S8 Limits on the planing margins and if deviation from the stated sizes is not permitted S9 Method of jointing or form of construction where not at the discretion of the Contractor

CLASSIFICATION TABLE

Classification	Sub-classification		Unit		MEASUREMENT RULES	DEFINITION RULES	COVERAGE RULES
1 Trusses 2 Trussed rafters 3 Trussed beams 4 Wall or partition panels 5 Portal frames	1 Dimensioned description		nr	1 Stopped labours (nr)			C2 The work is deemed to include webs, gussets, etc.
6 Floor members 7 Wall or partition members 8 Plates	1 Dimensioned description		m	1 Length > 6.00 m in one continuous length, length stated		D2 Floor members include joists and beams D3 Partition members include struts and noggings D4 Plates are those to structural elements only and include bearers	
9 Roof members	1 Flat 2 Pitched		m			D5 Flat roof members include joists and beams D6 Pitched roof members include struts, purlins, rafters, hip and valley rafters, ridge boards, ceiling joists, binders and bracing	
10 Joist strutting	1 Herringbone, depth of joist stated 2 Block, depth of joist stated		m		M1 Strutting is measured over the joists		
11 Butt jointed supports 12 Framed supports	1 Width > 300 mm	1 Dimensioned overall cross-section description and spacing of the members	m²	1 Different cross-section shapes (nr)	M2 Supports and framed supports are measured overall	D7 Supports include grounds, battens, firrings, fillets, drips, rolls, upstands, kerbs or the like	
	2 Width ≤ 300 mm		m	2 Curved, radii stated 3 Stopped labours (nr)			
13 Individual supports	1 Dimensioned overall cross-section description		m	4 Irregular component, details stated 5 Irregular shaped area		D8 Framed supports are where the members are jointed together other than butt jointed	

	2 Dimensioned overall cross-section description		Unit	Rules
	3 Width ≤ 300 mm			D10 Fascia boards include barge boards
16 Eaves or verge soffit boards				
17 Cleats	1 Dimensioned description		nr	D11 Cleats include sprockets and the like
18 Ornamental ends				
19 Wrot surfaces	1 Plain	1 Width stated	m	D12 Wrot surfaces are those on sawn items only
	2 Irregular	1 Girth stated		
20 Straps	1 Dimensioned description		nr	D13 Bolts include heads, nuts and washers
21 Hangers	2 Dimensioned diagram			M4 The length of a bolt is measured overall the head
22 Shoes				C3 Work is deemed to include all labours in fabricating and fixing
23 Nail plates				C4 Work is deemed to include all accessories
24 Metal connectors				
25 Bolts				
26 Rod bracing				
27 Wire bracing				
28 Others, details stated				

grouped together

G30 Metal profiled sheet decking

INFORMATION PROVIDED

P1 The following information is shown either on drawings under A Preliminaries/General conditions or on further drawings which accompany the bills of quantities:
(a) the extent of the work and its height above ground level
(b) the size of units where not at the discretion of the Contractor

CLASSIFICATION TABLE

			MEASUREMENT RULES	DEFINITION RULES	COVERAGE RULES	SUPPLEMENTARY INFORMATION
				D1 All sizes are nominal sizes unless stated as finished sizes	C1 Removal of lifting devices and consequent making good and making good of handling holes and the like are deemed to be included	S1 Kind and quality of materials S2 Method of fixing and hoisting where not at the discretion of the Contractor S3 Method of jointing or form of construction where not at the discretion of the Contractor S4 Surface treatments applied as part of the production process
1 Decking 2 Decking units (nr)	1 Dimensioned description	m²	1 Curved, radii stated 2 Fixing through underlinings	M1 The number is stated only where the size of unit is not at the discretion of the Contractor		
3 Items extra over the decking or decking units in which they occur	1 Holes 2 Notches 3 Others, details stated	nr		M2 No deduction is made for voids ≤ 0.50 m²		
4 Bearings 5 Eaves 6 Kerbs 7 Abutments 8 Nibs 9 Blocks 10 Fillets 11 Profile fillers	1 Dimensioned description	m				

INFORMATION PROVIDED	MEASUREMENT RULES	DEFINITION RULES	COVERAGE RULES	SUPPLEMENTARY INFORMATION
P1 The following information is shown either on location drawings under A Preliminaries/General conditions or on further drawings which accompany the bills of quantities: (a) the extent of the work and its height above ground level (b) the size of units where not at the discretion of the Contractor		D1 All sizes are nominal sizes unless stated as finished sizes	C1 Removal of lifting devices and consequent making good, and making good of handling holes and the like are deemed to be included	

CLASSIFICATION TABLE

				MEASUREMENT RULES	DEFINITION RULES	COVERAGE RULES	SUPPLEMENTARY INFORMATION
1 Decking 2 Decking units (nr)	1 Dimensioned description	m²	1 Curved, radii stated	M1 The number is stated only where the size of unit is not at the discretion of the Contractor			S1 Kind and quality of materials and whether sawn or wrot
3 Items extra over the decking or decking units in which they occur	1 Holes 2 Notches 3 Others, details stated	nr	1 Off site 2 On site	M2 No deduction is made for voids ≤ 0.50 m²			S2 Method of fixing and hoisting where not at the discretion of the Contractor
4 Woodwool kerbs 5 Woodwool angle fillets 6 Filling rebates with insulating strips 7 Isolating strips	1 Dimensioned description	m		M3 Items 4-7. *. 0. * are only measured under Section G32			S3 Method of jointing or form of construction where not at the discretion of the Contractor
							S4 Selection and protection for subsequent treatment
							S5 Surface treatments applied as part of the production process
							S6 Matching grain or colour
							S7 Limits on the planing margins and if deviation from the stated sizes is not permitted

H Cladding/Covering

H10 Patent glazing
H12 Plastics glazed vaulting/walling
H13 Structural glass assemblies

INFORMATION PROVIDED				MEASUREMENT RULES	DEFINITION RULES	COVERAGE RULES	SUPPLEMENTARY INFORMATION
P1 The following information is shown either on location drawings under A Preliminaries/General conditions or on further drawings which accompany the bills of quantities: (a) the scope and location of the work (b) component drawings				M1 No deduction is made for voids ≤ 1.00 m²			S1 Kind, quality and thickness of materials S2 Type, finish, length and spacing of glazing members S3 Nature, thickness and spacing of structural supports
CLASSIFICATION TABLE							
1 Roofs areas (nr) 2 Vertical surfaces (nr)	m²		1 Site drilling the bearings	M2 Glazing is measured over bars		C1 Work is deemed to include securing to wood unless otherwise stated	
3 Items extra over the glazing in which they occur	nr	1 Dimensioned description	1 Control gear to single unit, type, method of fixing and distance vertically and horizontally from unit stated 2 Control gear to bank of units, type, method of fixing and distance vertically and horizontally from units stated				
1 Doors 2 Windows 3 Fixed louvres 4 Adjustable louvres 5 Others, details stated							
4 Raking cutting 5 Curved cutting	m			M3 Labours on glazing are grouped with the glazing to which they relate			
6 Weatherings, flashings and fixing members at tops, bottoms and sides where part of the component	m	1 Dimensioned description 1 Preformed, gauge stated 2 Extruded, thickness stated	1 Site drilling, background stated			C2 Stop ends, mitres and corners are deemed to be included	

P1 The following information is shown either on location drawings under A Preliminaries/General conditions or on further drawings which accompany the bills of quantities:
(a) the scope and location of the work
(b) component drawings

CLASSIFICATION TABLE

1 Curtain walling	1 Dimensioned description	m²	1 Flat
			2 Sloping
			3 Curved, radii stated
2 Items extra over the curtain walling in which they occur			
1 Infill panels	1 Type and thickness stated	m²	
2 Perimeter		m	1 Heads
			2 Sills
			3 Abutments
			1 Irregular
			2 Horizontal
			3 Sloping
			4 Vertical
			5 Curved, radii stated
3 Angle			1 Internal
			2 External
4 Closer			1 Fire stops
			2 Partition closer
			3 Angle closer
			4 Plaster stop
5 Opening lights	1 Dimensioned description	nr	
6 Doors			

M (Measurement rules)

M1 Timber members which do not have a constant cross-section are so described and given stating the extreme dimensions

M2 No deduction is made for voids ≤ 1.00 m²

M3 Infill panels are measured over all framing

D (Definition rules)

D1 Curtain walling comprises non loadbearing walls of wood or metal framing, fixed as an intergrated assembly, complete with windows and opening lights, glazing and infill panels

D2 All sizes are nominal sizes unless stated as finished sizes

D3 Irregular junctions are any junctions with angles other than 90°

D4 Opening lights include opening gear as appropriate

C (Coverage rules)

C1 Curtain walling is deemed to include all cleats, brackets, bolts and fixings

C2 Items include:
(a) doors where supplied with the unit
(b) architraves, trims and the like where part of the component
(c) ironmongery where supplied with the component
(d) finishes where part of the component as delivered
(e) glazing where supplied with the component
(f) mechanical operation and automatic operating equipment where supplied with the component
(g) mastics/sealants unless executed by a specialist and measured in Section P22
(h) fixings and fastenings

Supplementary information

S1 Kind and quality of materials and if timber whether sawn or wrot

S2 Preservative treatments applied as part of the production process

S3 Surface treatments applied as part of the production process

S4 Selection and protection for subsequent treatment

S5 Matching grain or colour

S6 Limits on planing margins on timber and if deviation from stated size is not permitted

S7 Method of jointing or form of construction

S8 Thickness or substance

S9 Method of fixing where not at the discretion of the Contractor

S10 Bedding and jointing or pointing compound

S11 Fixing through vulnerable materials

H14 Concrete rooflights/pavement lights

INFORMATION PROVIDED					MEASUREMENT RULES	DEFINITION RULES	COVERAGE RULES	SUPPLEMENTARY INFORMATION
P1 Information is shown on location drawings under A Preliminaries/General conditions								
CLASSIFICATION TABLE								
1 Rooflights 2 Pavement lights 3 Vertical units	1 Dimensioned description (nr)	1 Sizes and extent of reinforcement stated	m²		M1 Isolated glass lenses are measured in Section E42		C1 Roof and pavement lights are deemed to include moulds, formwork, reinforcement, bedding and glass lenses	S1 Kind and quality of materials S2 Bedding and fixing S3 Surface finishes
	2 Dimensioned description		nr					
4 Joints	1 Dimensioned description	1 Sizes of filling and sealants stated	m					

H20 Rigid sheet cladding
H21 Timber weatherboarding
H92 Rainscreen cladding
K11 Rigid sheet flooring/sheathing/decking/sarking/linings/casings
K12 Under purlin/inside rail panel linings
K13 Rigid sheet fine linings/panelling
K14 Glassfibre reinforced gypsum linings/panelling/casings/mouldings
K15 Vitreous enamel linings/panelling
K20 Timber board flooring/decking/sarking/linings/casings
K21 Timber strip/board fine flooring/linings

INFORMATION PROVIDED	MEASUREMENT RULES	DEFINITION RULES	COVERAGE RULES	SUPPLEMENTARY INFORMATION
P1 Information is shown on location drawings under A Preliminaries/General conditions	M1 No deduction is made for voids ≤ 0.50 m² M2 Work to ceilings and beams over 3.50 m above floor (measured to ceiling level in both cases), is so described stating the height in	D1 The work is deemed internal unless described as external D2 All sizes are nominal sizes unless stated as finished sizes D3 Timber items which do not have a constant cross	C1 The work is deemed to include: (a) labours, except as otherwise required (b) breather paper lining/sheathing (c) angles, except as otherwise required	

			1 Dimensioned description		
1 Walls	1 Width > 300 mm	m²	1 Laid diagonally	M3 Width stages are measured the width of each face	D4 Walls include jambs and cills to openings and recesses in walls and attached columns
2 Floors	2 Width ≤ 300 mm	m	2 Sloping		D5 Ceilings include soffits to openings and recesses in walls, all faces of recesses in ceilings and attached beams
3 Ceilings			3 Curved, radii stated		
4 Roofs	3 Area ≤ 1.00 m², irrespective of width	nr	4 Obstructed by integral services		
5 Tops and cheeks of dormers					D6 Sloping is defined as sloping both > 10° from horizontal and > 10° from vertical
6 Isolated beams	1 Total girth ≤ 600 mm	m²		M4 The girth is measured on the external finished face	
7 Isolated columns	2 and thereafter in 600 mm stages				D7 Isolated beams and isolated columns include the faces of attached beams and attached columns which have a different finish from the adjoining face
8 Abutments	1 Type stated	m			D8 Abutments are defined as being where the detail is different from the standard detail and (where appropriate) include around openings etc.
9 Finished angles	1 External	m			D9 Finished angles are those where the decorative veneer or facing is returned or on panelling where angles are other than butt jointed
	2 Internal				
10 Holes		nr			D10 Holes are those for pipes, standards and the like
11 Fire stops	1 Dimensioned description	m			
12 Items extra over the work in which they occur	1 Access panels	nr	1 Dimensioned description		

S1 Type, quality and thickness of materials and if timber whether sawn or wrot

S2 Method of jointing or form of construction where not at the discretion of the Contractor

S3 Nature of background

S4 Preservative treatments applied as part of the production process

S5 Surface treatments applied as part of the production process

S6 Fire retardant treatments

S7 Details of cover and jointing strips and cover mouldings

S8 Selection and protection for subsequent treatments

S9 Constraints on width of board and planing margins and limitations if deviation from stated sizes is not permitted

S10 Matching grain or colour

S11 Fixing through vulnerable materials

S12 Method of fixing where not at the discretion of the Contractor

S13 Details of finish, trim or support

H30 Fibre cement profiled sheet cladding/covering/siding

H31 Metal profiled sheet cladding/covering/siding

H32 Plastics profiled sheet cladding/covering/siding

H33 Bitumen and fibre profiled sheet cladding/covering

H41 Glassfibre reinforced plastics panel cladding/features

H43 Metal panel cladding/features

INFORMATION PROVIDED			MEASUREMENT RULES	DEFINITION RULES	COVERAGE RULES	SUPPLEMENTARY INFORMATION
P1 The following information is shown either on location drawings under A Preliminaries/General conditions or on further drawings which accompany the bills of quantities: (a) the extent of the work and its height above ground level						S1 Kind, quality and size of materials S2 Type and spacing of fixing
CLASSIFICATION TABLE						
1 Roof coverings 2 Wall cladding	m²	1 Curved, radii stated 2 Fixed through underlinings	M1 No deduction is made for voids ≤ 1.00 m²		C1 Coverings are deemed to include: (a) work in forming voids ≤ 1.00 m² other than holes (b) integral underlay	S3 Minimum side and end laps S4 Jointing or sealing S5 Nature, thickness and spacing of structural supports
3 Abutments 4 Eaves 5 Verges 6 Ridges 7 Hips 8 Vertical angles 9 Valleys 10 Expansion joints 11 Barge boards 12 Skirtings 13 Flashings 14 Aprons/sills 15 Gutters and linings 16 Jambs 17 Filler pieces	m	1 Dimensioned cross-section description	1 Raking 2 Curved, radii stated	M2 Boundary work to voids is only measured where the void is > 1.00 m²		C2 Boundary work is deemed to include bedding, pointing, ends, angles and intersections	

cladding		3 Rooflight units		
		4 Sheets with louvre blades		
		5 Ventilators		
		6 Junctions		
20 Cutting	m	1 Raking		
		2 Curved		
21 Holes	nr		D1 Holes are those for pipes, standards and the like
22 Fire stops	m	1 Dimensioned description		

H51 Natural stone slab cladding/features
H52 Cast stone slab cladding/features

INFORMATION PROVIDED	MEASUREMENT RULES	DEFINITION RULES	COVERAGE RULES	SUPPLEMENTARY INFORMATION
P1 The following information is shown either on location drawings under A Preliminaries/General conditions or on further drawings which accompany the bills of quantities: (a) the scope and location of the work	M1 Work is measured on the exposed face and no deduction is made for voids ≤ 0.50 m² M2 Work in staircase areas and plant rooms are each given separately M3 Work to ceilings and beams over 3.50 m above floor (measured to ceiling level in both cases), except in staircase areas, is so described stating the height in further 1.50 m stages M4 Curved work is so described with the radii stated measured on face	D1 All work is deemed external unless described as internal D2 The thickness stated is the thickness exclusive of keys, grooves and the like D3 Rounded internal and external angles > 10 mm radius are classified as curved work where not measured under 15.1.∗.0	C1 The work is deemed to include: (a) fair joints (b) working over and around obstructions (c) additional labour for overhand work (d) cutting (e) drainage holes (f) bedding mortars and adhesives (g) grouting (h) cleaning, sealing and polishing	S1 Kind and quality of materials S2 Size, shape and thickness of units S3 Nature of base S4 Preparatory work S5 Nature of finished surface including any sealing/polishing S6 Bedding or other method of fixing S7 Treatment of joints S8 Layout of joints

CLASSIFICATION TABLE

				MEASUREMENT RULES	DEFINITION RULES	COVERAGE RULES	
1 Walls	1 Plain, width > 300 mm		m²	M5 Width is the width of each face	D4 Beams and columns are classified as isolated where the work is different from the abutting ceilings or walls D5 Work to sides and soffits of attached beams and openings and to sides of attached columns is classed as work to the abutting walls or ceilings	C2 Work to walls, ceilings, beams and columns is deemed to include internal and external angles and intersections ≤ 10 mm radius	
2 Ceilings	2 Plain, width ≤ 300 mm		m				
3 Isolated beams	3 Work with joints laid out to detail, width > 300 mm	1 Dimensioned description	m²				
4 Isolated columns	4 Work with joints laid out to detail, width ≤ 300 mm		m				
		1 Patterned, details stated					
5 Floors	1 Level or to falls only ≤ 15° from horizontal	1 Plain	m²		D6 Floors include landings	C3 Work to floors is deemed to include intersections in sloping work	
	2 To falls and crossfalls and to slopes ≤ 15° from horizontal	2 Work with joints laid out to detail, dimensioned diagram stated					
	3 To slopes > 15° from horizontal	1 Patterned work, details stated 2 Floors laid in bays, average size of bays stated 3 Inserts, size or section stated					

Item	Classification	Classification	Classification	Unit	Rules
8 Risers	1 Plain; 2 Undercut	1 Height stated		m	C5 Curved treads, risers, strings and aprons are deemed to include curved and radiused cutting for special edge tiles
9 Strings; 10 Aprons		1 Girth on face stated		m	C6 Strings and aprons are deemed to include fair edges, ends, angles and ramps
11 Linings to channels	1 Horizontal; 2 To falls	1 Height stated		m	C7 Linings to channels are deemed to include arrises, coves, ends, angles, intersections and outlets
12 Skirtings; 13 Kerbs	1 Height stated; 2 Height and width stated	1 Patterned work, details stated; 2 Inserts, size or section stated; 3 Flush; 4 Raking; 5 Vertical		m	C8 Skirtings and kerbs are deemed to include fair edges, rounded edges, ends, angles and ramps
14 Corner pieces	1 Dimensioned description	1 Dimensioned description		nr	
15 Items extra over the work in which they occur	1 Special units; 2 Access units; 3 Isolated special units	2 Manufacturer's reference		m / nr	D7 Special units include non-standard units to produce fair edges, internal and external angles, moulded edges, beaded edges, and coved junctions
16 Accessories	1 Separating membranes, thickness stated			m²	
	2 Movement joints; 3 Cover strips; 4 Dividing strips	1 Dimensioned description		m	D8 Movement joints include expansion joints
	5 Ornaments, dimensioned description and character stated	1 In situ; 2 Precast	1 Undercut	nr	D9 Ornaments are irregularly occurring features
	6 Fixings, details stated			nr	S9 Method of fixing

H60 Plain roof tiling
H61 Fibre cement slating
H62 Natural slating
H63 Reconstructed stone slating/tiling
H64 Timber shingling
H65 Single lap roof tiling
H66 Bituminous felt shingling

INFORMATION PROVIDED				MEASUREMENT RULES	DEFINITION RULES	COVERAGE RULES	SUPPLEMENTARY INFORMATION
P1 The following information is shown either on location drawings under A Preliminaries/General conditions or on further drawings which accompany the bills of quantities: (a) the extent of the roofing work and its height above ground level							S1 Kind, quality and size of materials S2 Method of fixing

CLASSIFICATION TABLE

				MEASUREMENT RULES	DEFINITION RULES	COVERAGE RULES	SUPPLEMENTARY INFORMATION
1 Root coverings 2 Wall coverings	1 Pitch stated	1 Curved, radii stated	m²	M1 No deduction is made for voids ≤ 1.00 m²		C1 Coverings are deemed to include: (a) underlay and battens (b) work in forming voids ≤ 1.00 m² other than holes	S3 Minimum laps S4 Spacing of battens and counter battens
3 Abutments 4 Eaves 5 Verges		1 Raking 2 Curved, radii stated	m	M2 Boundary work to voids is only measured where the void is > 1.00 m²		C2 Boundary work is deemed to include undercloaks, cutting, bedding, pointing, ends, angles and intersections	S5 Method of forming
6 Ridges 7 Hips 8 Vertical angles 9 Valleys							
10 Fittings 1 Ventilators 2 Finials 3 Gas terminals 4 Hip irons 5 Soakers 6 Saddles	1 Dimensioned description	1 Fixing only	nr				
11 Holes			nr		D1 Holes are those for pipes, standards and the like		

H70 Malleable metal sheet prebonded coverings/cladding
H71 Lead sheet coverings/flashings
H72 Aluminium strip/sheet coverings/flashings
H73 Copper strip/sheet coverings/flashings
H74 Zinc strip/sheet coverings/flashings
H75 Stainless steel strip/sheet coverings/flashings
H76 Fibre bitumen thermoplastic sheet coverings/flashings

INFORMATION PROVIDED	MEASUREMENT RULES	DEFINITION RULES	COVERAGE RULES	SUPPLEMENTARY INFORMATION
P1 The following information is shown either on location drawings under A Preliminaries/General conditions or on further drawings which accompany the bills of quantities: (a) the extent of the roofing work and its height above ground level (b) the location and spacing of all laps, drips, welts, cross welts, beads, seams, rolls, upstands and downstands				S1 Type and quality of materials for backing, underlays, coverings, cladding and flashings S2 Thickness, weight and temper grade S3 Method of fixing S4 Details of laps, drips, welts, beads, rolls, joints, upstands and downstands S5 Type of support materials S6 Special finishes

CLASSIFICATION TABLE

INFORMATION PROVIDED		MEASUREMENT RULES	DEFINITION RULES	COVERAGE RULES	SUPPLEMENTARY INFORMATION
1 Roof coverings 2 Wall coverings 3 Preformed cladding panels 4 Dormers 5 Hoods 6 Domes 7 Spires 8 Finials 9 Soffits	1 Pitch stated	m²	1 Curved, radii stated	M1 No deduction is made for voids ≤ 1.00 m² M2 The following allowances are made in calculating the area to be measured: (a) 180 mm for each drip < 50 mm high (b) 80 mm for each welt (c) 250 mm for each roll < 50 mm high (d) 100 mm for each seam (e) 500 mm for each lap (f) 500 mm for each upstand/downstand	C1 Coverings are deemed to include: (a) isolated areas (b) work to falls and crossfalls (c) underlay in contact with the covering (d) work in forming voids ≤ 1.00 m² other than holes (e) dressing/wedging into grooves, hollows, recesses and the like

H70/H71/H72/H73/H74/H75/H76 continued

CLASSIFICATION TABLE		Unit			MEASUREMENT RULES	DEFINITION RULES	COVERAGE RULES	SUPPLEMENTARY INFORMATION
10 Flashings 11 Aprons 12 Sills 13 Weatherings 14 Cappings 15 Hips 16 Kerbs 17 Ridges 18 Reveals, returns and jambs	1 Dimensioned description 2 Dimensioned diagram	m	1 Horizontal 2 Sloping 3 Vertical 4 Stepped 5 Preformed 6 Dressing over corrugated roofing 7 Dressing over slating and tiling 8 Dressing over glass and glazing bars		M3 Boundary work to voids is only measured where the void is > 1.00 m²		C2 Work is deemed to include: (a) laps, seams, ends (b) angles and intersections (c) rolls (d) upstands and downstands (e) dressing/wedging into grooves, hollows, recesses and the like	
19 Gutters		nr	1 Stepped 2 Secret 3 Sloping 4 Tapered 5 Preformed					
20 Catchpits 21 Sumps 22 Outlets	1 Dimensioned description	nr						
23 Edges	1 Welted 2 Beaded 3 Shaped	m						
24 Dressings	1 Corrugated roofing 2 Slating and tiling 3 Glass and glazing bars	m	1 Nature of roofing	1 Down corrugations 2 Across corrugations				
25 Saddles 26 Soakers and slates 27 Hatch covers 28 Ventilators	1 Dimensioned description	nr	1 Handed to others for fixing					
29 Collars around pipes, standards and the like	1 Size of member and length of collar stated					D1 Collars include pipe sleeves	C3 All dressing and bossing is deemed included	
30 Holes		nr				D2 Holes are those for		

J Waterproofing

J20 Mastic asphalt tanking/damp proofing
J21 Mastic asphalt roofing/insulation/finishes
J22 Proprietary roof decking with asphalt finish
J30 Liquid applied tanking/damp proofing
J31 Liquid applied waterproof roof coatings
M11 Mastic asphalt flooring/floor underlays

		MEASUREMENT RULES	DEFINITION RULES	COVERAGE RULES	SUPPLEMENTARY INFORMATION
INFORMATION PROVIDED					
P1 The following information is shown either on location drawings under A Preliminaries/General conditions or on further drawings which accompany the bills of quantities: (a) plan of each level indicating the extent of the work and its height above ground level together with restrictions on the siting of plant and materials (b) section indicating the extent of tanking work		M1 Mastic asphalt flooring in staircase areas and plant areas and plant rooms are each given separately M2 Curved work is so described	D1 Mastic asphalt flooring is deemed internal unless described as external	C1 Work is deemed to include: (a) cutting to line (b) cutting, notching, bending and extra material for lapping the underlay and reinforcement (c) working into recessed duct covers and the like, shaped insets, recessed manhole covers, mat sinkings, outlet pipes, dishing to gullies and the like (d) work to falls and crossfalls	S1 Kind, quality and size of materials including underlays and reinforcement S2 Thickness and number of coats S3 Nature of base on which applied S4 Surface treatments S5 Method of fixing decking S6 Spacing of structural supports

CLASSIFICATION TABLE							
1 Tanking and damp proofing	1 Width ≤ 150 mm	1 Pitch stated	m²	1 Work subsequently covered	M3 The area measured is that in contact with the base and no deduction is made for voids ≤ 1.00 m²		C2 Work is deemed to include: (a) working to metal or other flashings and working against frames of manhole covers, duct covers and the like (b) intersections on work to crossfalls C3 Work subsequently covered is deemed to include edges and arises
2 Flooring and underlay	2 Width 150 – 225 mm			2 Carried out in working space ≤ 600 mm wide			
3 Roofing	3 Width 225 – 300 mm			3 Overhand work			
4 Paving	4 Width > 300 mm						

Classification	Supplementary information	Unit	Measurement rules	Coverage/Definition rules
7 Aprons	3 Girth 225 – 300 mm 4 Girth > 300 mm girth stated		3 Raking in two planes	...internal angle-fillets, dressing over tilting fillets, turning nibs into grooves, angles, stopped ends requiring angle fillets, stopped ends, fair ends, and extra materials for turning into grooves
8 Linings to gutters 9 Linings to channels 10 Linings to valleys 11 Coverings to kerbs				C5 Linings to gutters, channels and valleys and coverings to kerbs are deemed to include edges, arrises, internal angle-fillets, tilting fillets, turning nibs into grooves, ends, angles, intersections, outlets and extra material for turning into grooves
12 Internal angle fillets	1 Dimensioned description	m	M5 Boundary work to voids is only measured where the void is > 1.00 m²	C6 Internal angle fillets are deemed to include ends and angles
13 Fair edges 14 Rounded edges 15 Drips 16 Arrises 17 Turning asphalt nibs into grooves		m	1 Coats (nr) where other than two	M6 12–17.*.0.* are only measured in association with work measured under 1–4.*.1.* M7 Edges and arrises are only measured separately where the work is not subsequently covered
18 Collars around pipes, standards and like members	1 Size of member and length of collar stated	nr		C7 Collars around pipes, standards and the like are deemed to include arrises and internal angle fillets D2 Collars include pipe sleeves
19 Linings to cesspools 20 Linings to sumps 21 Linings to manholes	1 Dimensioned description	nr		C8 Linings to cesspools, sumps and the like are deemed to include arrises, internal angle-fillets and outlets
22 Edge trim		m		C9 Edge trim is deemed to include ends, angles and intersections D3 Edge trim includes preformed angle trim
23 Roof ventilators		nr		

J40 Flexible sheet tanking/damp proofing
J41 Built up felt roof coverings
J42 Single layer polymeric roof coverings
J43 Proprietary roof decking with felt finish
J44 Sheet linings for pools/lakes/waterways

INFORMATION PROVIDED				MEASUREMENT RULES	DEFINITION RULES	COVERAGE RULES	SUPPLEMENTARY INFORMATION
P1 The following information is shown either on location drawings under A Preliminaries/General conditions or on further drawings which accompany the bills of quantities: (a) plan at each level indicating the extent of the work and its height above ground level together with restrictions on the siting of plant and materials				M1 Curved work is so described with the radii stated		C1 Work is deemed to include: (a) cutting and fair edges (b) notching, bending and extra material for laps	S1 Kind, quality and size of materials including underlays S2 Nature of base on which applied S3 Method of jointing S4 Method of fixing decking S5 Spacing of structural supports
CLASSIFICATION TABLE							
1 Tanking and damp proofing 2 Roof coverings 3 Sheet linings to pools, lakes or waterways		m²	1 Curved radii stated	M2 The area measured is that in contact with the base and no deduction is made for voids ≤ 1.00 m²		C2 Boundary work is deemed to include all cutting, ends, angles, intersections, notching, bending, turning into grooves, wedging, dressing, trimming and jointing covering to flashings, working into channels and the like and filler pieces	
4 Abutments 5 Eaves 6 Verges 7 Ridges 8 Hips 9 Vertical angles 10 Valleys 11 Skirtings 12 Flashings 13 Aprons 14 Gutters and linings 15 Coverings to kerbs		m² / m	1 Girth > 2.00 m	2 Girth ≤ 2.00 m in 200 mm stages	M3 Boundary work to voids is only measured where the void is > 1.00 m²			
16 Linings to cesspools 17 Linings to sumps	1 Dimensioned description	nr					
18 Collars around pipes, standards and the like	1 Size of pipe and length of collar stated				D1 Collars include pipe sleeves		
19 Outlets and dishing to gullies	1 Dimensioned description						

		Unit	
21	Roof ventilators	nr	
22	Holes	nr	D3 Holes are those for pipes, standards and the like
23	Fire stops	m	1 Dimensioned description

K Linings/Sheathing/Dry partitioning

K10 Plasterboard dry linings/partitions/ceilings

INFORMATION PROVIDED	MEASUREMENT RULES	DEFINITION RULES	COVERAGE RULES	SUPPLEMENTARY INFORMATION
P1 The following information is shown either on location drawings under A Preliminaries/General conditions or on further drawings which accompany the bills of quantities: (a) the scope and location of the work (b) the services located within the ceiling or partition where the work includes complex integral services	M1 Work in staircase areas and plant rooms are each given separately M2 Work to ceilings and beams over 3.50 m above floor (measured to ceiling level in both cases), except in staircase areas, is so described stating the height in further 1.50 m stages. M3 Insulation, vapour barriers, fire barriers, isolating membranes, moisture resistant treatment and the like, are only measured in this section where they are an integral part of a lining, or partition or ceiling, or are fixed thereto	D1 Work is deemed internal unless described as external	C1 Work is deemed to include: (a) fair joints (b) working over and around obstructions into recesses and shaped inserts (c) additional labour for overhand work (d) plaster for dabs, filling and finishing (e) joint and reinforcing tape (f) bitumen impregnated pads C2 Patterned work is deemed to include all extra work involved	S1 Kind, quality and thickness of sheeting and components S2 Method of construction S3 Layout and treatment of joints S4 Complex integral services S5 Method of fixing S6 Thermal insulation and vapour barriers fixed with lining S7 Insulation to limit sound transmission S8 Moisture resistant treatment and the like S9 Surface applications forming part of dry lining finish S10 Isolating membranes S11 Method of jointing composite panels

Item	First division	Second division	Third division	Unit	Measurement rules	Definition rules	Coverage rules	Supplementary information
1 Proprietary partitions	1 Height in 300 mm stages and thickness of partition stated	1 Boarded one side 2 Boarded both sides	1 Patterned, details stated 2 Curved, radii stated 3 Obstructed by integral services	m	M4 The work is measured over obstructions M5 No allowance is made in measurement for lapped joints M6 The linear measurement of partitions is the mean length of the partition	D2 The height of framed work is the height of the frame and where the heights of the boarding differ then this is so stated giving details	C3 Partitions and linings are deemed to include the following where part of the proprietary system. Where not a part of the proprietary system they are measured in accordance with the appropriate Work Section rules: (a) head and sole plates (b) studs, stiffening sections, firrings and channels (c) metal resilient bars (d) jointing battens (e) insulation and barriers (f) fillets, battens and the like	
2 Linings	1 Walls	1 Height in 300 mm stages stated		m	M7 The linear measurement of linings is the length on face	D3 Reveals and soffits of openings and recesses in linings > 600 mm are defined as to walls, beams or columns		
	2 Beams, faces (nr)	1 Total girth ≤ 600 mm			M8 No deduction is made for voids in partitions and linings measured linearly other than for those voids which extend full height, full girth or full width	D4 Linings are those which do not form part of a proprietary system and exclude timber framing		
	3 Columns, faces (nr)	2 and thereafter in 600 mm stages						
	4 Reveals and soffits of openings and recesses	1 Width ≤ 300 mm 2 Width 300 – 600 mm			M9 No deduction is made for voids ≤ 0.50 m² in linings measured superficially M10 Where one face of a double sided partition or a face of lining is carried across the surface of an obstruction, the partition or lining is measured overall and no item of abutments is measured M11 A recess is only measured where it is for part only of the height and not where it is full height			
	5 Ceilings			m²				
3 Angles to partitions 4 Tee junctions to partitions 5 Crosses to partitions	1 Plain 2 Irregular	1 Thickness of partition stated	1 Between different forms of construction, finish details stated	m			C4 Angles, tee junctions, crosses and abutments are deemed to include the extra work involved, studding, grounds, angle tapes and the like	S12 Detail of finish or trim, grounds or framing
6 Abutments	1 Thickness of partition or lining stated			m		D5 Abutments include trimming to openings which extend full height, full girth or full width unless finished with the same finish as the faces. Trimming to openings which are not full height, full girth or full width are deemed to be included		
7 Angles to linings	1 Internal 2 External	1 Between different board finishes, details stated		m			C5 Angles are deemed to include the extra work involved, angle tapes and the like	

K10 continued

CLASSIFICATION TABLE			MEASUREMENT RULES	DEFINITION RULES	COVERAGE RULES	SUPPLEMENTARY INFORMATION
8 Fair ends to partitions	1 Thickness of partition stated	m	M12 Fair ends are only measured where the exposed end of the partition is finished with the same finish as the faces, or with a trim which is an integral part of the partition system	D6 Fair ends to partitions include trimming to openings	C6 Fair ends are deemed to include the extra work involved, studding, boarding, trims and the like	S13 Details of finish or trim
9 Beads, function stated	1 Dimensioned description	m		D7 The function of beads as angle beads, casing beads, trims and the like are stated	C7 Beads are deemed to include working finishes thereto	
10 Fixings for heavy fittings	1 Sinks 2 Radiators 3 Cupboards 4 Others, details stated	nr		D8 Heavy fittings are those requiring additional support	C8 Fixings for heavy fittings are deemed to include additional supports and any cutting of boarding, trim or jointing	S14 Type of additional supports
11 Items extra over the work in which they occur	1 Access panels	nr				S15 Type of panels

P1 The following information is shown either on location drawings under A Preliminaries/General conditions or on further drawings which accompany the bills of quantities:
(a) the scope and location of the work
(b) the services located within the partition

D1 Work is deemed internal unless described as external

CLASSIFICATION TABLE

				Measurement Rules	Definition Rules	Coverage Rules	Information
1 Partitions	Height and thickness of partition stated	1 Factory applied finish 2 Site applied finish	1 Curved, radii stated 2 Obstructed by integral services	m	M1 The work is measured over the obstructions M2 The linear measurement of partitions is the mean length of the partition M3 Factory applied finishes and site applied finishes are only measured where not at the discretion of the Contractor		C1 Partitions are deemed to include all integral components, holes, etc preformed at factory but excluding trim	S1 Kind and quality of materials S2 Method of construction S3 Layout of joints S4 Method of fixing S5 Complex integral services
2 Trims	1 Dimensioned description			m		D2 Trims are separate items fixed on site as cover pieces to edges or panel joints		
3 Openings, extra over the partitions in which they occur 1 Blanks 2 Doors 3 Windows 4 Glazed panels 5 Access panels	1 Dimensioned description			nr		D3 Openings is a general term for breaks in the general construction of partitions and includes the components filling the openings	C2 Openings are deemed to include additional integral components C3 Openings are deemed to include ironmongery, glass, linings or the like but exclude trim	S6 Method of bedding, jointing or pointing S7 Details of ironmongery, glass, linings or the like

K32 Panel cubicles

	MEASUREMENT RULES	DEFINITION RULES	COVERAGE RULES	SUPPLEMENTARY INFORMATION
INFORMATION PROVIDED				
P1 The following information is shown either on location drawings under A Preliminaries/General conditions or on further drawings which accompany the bills of quantities: (a) the scope and location of the work				
CLASSIFICATION TABLE				
1 Cubicle partitions; set 1 Dimensioned diagram nr		D1 Cubicle sets include doors, ironmongery or the like but exclude trims	C1 Cubicle sets are deemed to include framing, stiffening, connecting and fixing devices supportings legs and brackets	S1 Kind and quality of materials S2 Method of construction S3 Method of fixing S4 Method of bedding, jointing or pointing
2 Trim 1 Dimensioned description m		D2 Trims refer to separate items fixed on site at junction of cubicles and at junctions with adjoining constructions		

INFORMATION

S1 Kind and quality of materials
S2 Size of panels and strips
S3 Construction of framing and suspension systems
S4 Method of fixing
S5 Nature of backgrounds
S6 Services in the suspended ceiling void
S7 Insulation materials
S8 Vapour barriers
S9 Integral heating, ventilation, lighting and fire prevention fittings
S10 Composition of panels and method of fixing
S11 Method of support and depth of suspension

Coverage rules

C1 Suspended ceilings etc. are deemed to include:
(a) working over and around obstructions
(b) support work and accessories for fittings
(c) suspension and framed members
C2 Patterned work is deemed to include all extra work involved
C3 Work incorporating integral fittings is deemed to include additional hangers, framing and the like
C4 Access panels are deemed to include edge trim and fixings

Definition rules

D1 All work is deemed internal unless described as external
D2 Integral fittings occur where the fittings are designed and incorporated into the ceiling structure
D3 Isolated strips of ceiling are those which are narrower than the specified relevant lining unit dimension

Measurement rules

M1 Soffit linings on battens, etc. fixed direct to underside of slab are measured elsewhere in the relevant Sections
M2 Work in staircase areas and plant rooms are each given separately
M3 Work to ceilings and beams over 3.50 m above floor (measured to ceiling level in both cases), except in staircase areas, is so described stating the height in further 1.50 m stages
M4 The area measured is that on the exposed face and no deduction is made for voids ≤ 0.50 m²
M5 The depth of suspension is measured from the main structural soffit to the lining
M6 Insulation and vapour barriers are measured in this Section where they are an integral part of the ceiling and are fixed in the ceiling
M7 Isolated strips of ceilings are not measured separately between the boundary of the lining and the first line of integral fittings

P1 The following information is shown either on location drawings under A Preliminaries/General conditions or on further drawings which accompany the bills of quantities:
(a) the scope and location of the work including integral fittings
(b) the services located within the suspended ceiling void including any additional support for same

CLASSIFICATION TABLE

		Unit		
1 Ceilings 2 Beams	1 Depth of suspension ≤ 150 mm 2 Depth of suspension 150 – 500 mm 3 and thereafter in 500 mm stages	m²	1 Patterned, details stated 2 Sloping linings, details stated 3 Curved, radii stated 4 Suspension obstructed by services 5 Trims at regular intervals within area of suspended ceiling, details stated	1 Thickness of lining and method of fixing system to structure stated
3 Isolated strips of suspended ceiling, thickness of lining stated	1 Width ≤ 300 mm 2 and thereafter in 300 mm stages	m		
4 Items extra over the lining in which they occur	1 Access panels	nr	1 Dimensioned description	
5 Upstands	1 Height ≤ 300 mm 2 and thereafter in 300 mm stages	m		1 Thickness of lining

K40 continued

CLASSIFICATION TABLE		Unit	MEASUREMENT RULES	DEFINITION RULES	COVERAGE RULES	SUPPLEMENTARY INFORMATION
6 Irregular window and dormer cheeks	1 Dimensioned description	nr			C5 Irregular window and dormer cheeks are deemed to include cutting and extra supports	
7 Cavity fire barriers, total thickness stated	1 Plain 2 Obstructed by services	m	1 Height ≤ 300 mm 2 and thereafter in 300 mm stages		C6 Cavity fire barriers are deemed to include all scribing, angles, ends, and support work	
8 Edge trims	1 Dimensioned description	m	M8 Trims at regular intervals within the area of suspended ceiling are included within the item description of same 1–3.∗.∗.5 M9 Trims are measured to openings formed for fittings	D4 Plain edge trims are those which are fixed to the structure D5 Floating edge trims are those which are fixed to the ceiling system	C7 Trims are deemed to include mitred, regular and irregular angles	S12 Centres of fixing
9 Angle trims	1 Plain 2 Floating					
10 Items extra over the trims in which they occur	1 Irregular angle pieces	nr		D6 Irregular angle pieces are purpose made manufactured corner pieces		
11 Collars to services passing through fire barriers	1 Pipes 2 Trunking	nr	1 Length of sleeve each side of barrier stated	M10 Collars are measured where they are integral with fire barriers		S13 Types
12 Bridging	1 Span stated	m	1 Support to light fittings or the like M11 Bridging is measured where widths of trunking in the ceiling space obstruct the standard grid		C8 Bridging is deemed to include additional fixings	
13 Fittings	1 Dimensioned description	m nr				

P1 The following information is shown either on location drawings under A Preliminaries/General conditions or on further drawings which accompany the bills of quantities:
(a) the scope and location of the work

CLASSIFICATION TABLE

					Measurement rules	Coverage rules	Information
1 Floors	1 Thickness of panel stated	1 Height of cavity stated	m²	1 Patterned, details stated	M1 No deduction is made for voids ≤ 0.50 m²	C1 Raised access floors are deemed to include (a) panels, supporting structures, adhesives, bearing pads and the like (b) cutting and notching and extra supports	S1 Kind and quality of materials S2 Supporting systems S3 Frames to panels S4 Method of fixing
2 Ramps	1 Thickness, length and width stated		nr		M2 The height stated for ramps is the height at each end		
3 Items extra over the floors in which they occur	1 Special panels	1 Dimensioned description	nr				
4 Skirtings and perimeter edge trims	1 Dimensioned description		m		M3 Skirtings and perimeter edge trims not executed as part of the access floor are measured in Section P20	C2 Skirtings and perimeter edge trims are deemed to include ends and angles	

L Windows/Doors/Stairs

L10 Windows/Rooflights/Screens/Louvres

INFORMATION PROVIDED		MEASUREMENT RULES	DEFINITION RULES	COVERAGE RULES	SUPPLEMENTARY INFORMATION
P1 Information is shown on location drawings under A Preliminaries/General conditions			D1 All sizes of timber are nominal sizes unless stated as finished sizes		
CLASSIFICATION TABLE					
1 Windows and window frames	1 Dimensioned diagram nr	M1 Standard sections are identified		C1 The work is deemed to include notching around obstructions	S1 Kind and quality of materials and if timber whether sawn or wrot
2 Window shutters				C2 Items include:	S2 Preservatives treatment applied as part of the production process
3 Sun shields				(a) doors where supplied with the unit	
4 Rooflights, skylights, roof windows and frames				(b) architraves, trims, sills, subframes, and the like where part of the component	S3 Surface treatments applied as part of the production process
5 Screens, borrowed lights and frames				(c) ironmongery where supplied with the component	S4 Selection and protection for subsequent treatment
6 Shopfronts				(d) finishes where part of the component as delivered	S5 Matching grain or colour
7 Louvres and frames				(e) glazing where supplied with the component	S6 Limits on planing margins on timber and if deviation from stated size is not permitted
				(f) mechanical operation and automatic operating equipment where supplied with the component	S7 Method of jointing or form of construction
				(g) fixings and fastenings	S8 Method of fixing where not at the discretion of the Contractor
	m				S9 Fixing through vulnerable materials
8 Bedding frames					S10 Bedding, jointing and pointing compound
9 Pointing frames					
10 Bedding and pointing frames					

INFORMATION PROVIDED			MEASUREMENT RULES	DEFINITION RULES	COVERAGE RULES	SUPPLEMENTARY INFORMATION
P1 Information is shown on location drawings under A Preliminaries/General conditions				D1 All sizes of timber are nominal sizes unless stated as finished sizes		

CLASSIFICATION TABLE

Classification	Unit	Dimension / detail	MEASUREMENT RULES	COVERAGE RULES	SUPPLEMENTARY INFORMATION
1 Doors 2 Rolling shutters and collapsible gates 3 Sliding/folding partitions 4 Hatches 5 Strong room doors 6 Grilles	nr	1 Dimensioned diagram 1 Approximate weight stated	M1 Standard sections are identified M2 Each leaf of a multi-leafed door is counted as one door M3 Approximate weight is only stated for metal doors and includes their associated frames M4 Doors where supplied with their associated frames or linings are measured as composite items under General rule 9.1 M5 Enumerated composite door frame and lining sets need not state the number of sets within the description	C1 Doors are deemed to include fitting and hanging C2 The work is deemed to include notching around obstructions C3 Items include: (a) doors where supplied with the unit (b) architraves, trims and the like where part of the component (c) ironmongery where supplied with the component (d) finishes where part of the component as delivered (e) glazing where supplied with the component (f) mechanical operation and automatic operating equipment where supplied with the component (g) fixings and fastenings	S1 Kind and quality of materials and if timber whether sawn or wrot S2 Preservatives treatment applied as part of the production process S3 Surface treatments applied as part of the production process S4 Selection and protection for subsequent treatment S5 Matching grain or colour S6 Limits on planing margins on timber and if deviation from stated size is not permitted S7 Method of jointing or form of construction S8 Method of fixing where not at the discretion of the Contractor S9 Fixing through vulnerable materials S10 Bedding, jointing and pointing compound

7 Door frames and door linings, sets (nr)
  1 Jambs
  2 Heads
  3 Sills (nr)
  4 Mullions (nr)
  5 Transoms (nr)
	m	1 Dimensioned overall cross-section description
		1 Repeats of identical sets (nr)
		2 Different cross-section shapes (nr)
		3 Stopped labours (nr)			

6 Composite sets	nr	1 Dimensioned description			
8 Bedding frames 9 Pointing frames 10 Bedding and pointing frames	m				

L30 Stairs/Walkways/Balustrades
Q41 Barriers/Guardrails

INFORMATION PROVIDED			MEASUREMENT RULES	DEFINITION RULES	COVERAGE RULES	SUPPLEMENTARY INFORMATION
P1 Information is shown on location drawings under A Preliminaries/General conditions				D1 Work in this Section covers: (a) staircases, ladders and loft ladders (b) landings, catwalks and access walkways (c) balustrades and handrails (d) hatch doors where part of a loft ladder component		

CLASSIFICATION TABLE

			MEASUREMENT RULES	DEFINITION RULES	COVERAGE RULES	SUPPLEMENTARY INFORMATION
1 Composite item, type stated	1 Dimensioned description 2 Component drawing	nr	M1 Where accessories such as linings, trim nosings, ironmongery etc. are not included in a catalogue reference they are measured in the appropriate Work Sections M2 Isolated handrails are measured in Section P20		C1 Composite items are deemed to include: (a) linings, nosings, cover moulds, trims and the like where part of the component (b) soffit lining, spandrel panels and the like where part of the component (c) ironmongery and operating gear to loft ladders where supplied with the component (d) finishes where part of the component as delivered (e) fixings, fastenings, blockings, wedges, bolts, brackets, cleats and the like C2 Staircases are deemed to include newels	S1 Kind and quality of materials and if timber whether sawn or wrot S2 Preservative treatments applied as part of the production process S3 Surface treatments applied as part of the production process S4 Selection and protection for subsequent treatment S5 Matching grain or colour S6 Limits on planing margins on timber and if deviation from stated size is not permitted
2 Isolated balustrades 3 Associated handrails		m		D2 Isolated balustrades are those which do not form an integral part of a staircase unit D3 Associated handrails are handrails of a material different from the balustrade with which they are associated	C3 Plain ends are deemed to be included	S7 Method of jointing or form of construction S8 Method of fixing where not at the discretion of the Contractor S9 Fixing through vulnerable materials
4 Extra over the isolated balustrades or associated handrails in which they occur	1 Ramps 2 Wreaths 3 Bends 4 Ornamental ends	nr	1 Curved, radii stated			

L40 General glazing

INFORMATION PROVIDED			MEASUREMENT RULES	DEFINITION RULES	COVERAGE RULES	SUPPLEMENTARY INFORMATION
P1 Information is shown on location drawings under A Preliminaries/General conditions			M1 Each pane is measured separately for multiple glazed panes where not in sealed units M2 Labours on edges of glass louvre panes are given in the description	D1 Multiple glazed panes are the constituent panes of glazing of more than one layer		S1 Kind, quality and thickness of glass S2 Kind and quality of glazing compound – where more than single compound refer to 11.0.0.0 S3 Method of glazing S4 Method of securing including details of gaskets where gasket glazed S5 Nature of frame or surround

CLASSIFICATION TABLE

1 Standard plain glass	1 Glazing	1 Panes (nr), area ≤ 0.15 m² 2 Panes, area 0.15 – 4.00 m²	m²	M3 Panes of irregular shape are classified and measured according to the smallest rectangular area from which the pane can be obtained	D2 Standard plain glass is any glass (other than a special glass) which is ≤ 10 mm thick and in panes ≤ 4 m² and is not drilled, not brilliant cut and not bent	C1 Glazing is deemed to include raking and curved cutting	
		1 ≥ 50 identical panes (nr), size stated 2 Irregular shaped panes 3 Multiple glazed panes 4 Glazing rebates 20 – 30 mm 5 and thereafter in 10 mm stages 6 Panes required to align with adjacent panes					
	2 Louvres	1 Dimensioned description	nr				

L40 continued

CLASSIFICATION TABLE				MEASUREMENT RULES	DEFINITION RULES	COVERAGE RULES	SUPPLEMENTARY INFORMATION
2 Non-standard plain glass	1 Glazing 2 Louvres	nr	1 Dimensioned description	1 Multiple glazed panes 2 Glazing rebates 20–30 mm 3 and thereafter in 10 mm stages 4 Brilliant cut panes, type of decoration stated	D3 Non-standard plain glass is any glass (other than special glass) which is > 10 mm thick or is in panes > 4 m² or is drilled, brilliant cut or bent		
3 Special glass	1 Glazing 2 Louvres	nr		5 Bent in long dimension, radii stated 6 Bent in short dimension, radii stated 7 Bent in both dimensions, radii stated 8 Drilled panes, diameter, size and type of holes (nr) stated 9 Drilled panes with insulating sleeves, diameter, size and type of holes (nr) stated 10 Panes required to align with adjacent panes	D4 Special glass includes: (a) laminated (b) toughened (c) enamelled and toughened (d) bullet resistant (e) anti-bandit (f) solar control (g) sealed double glazing units (h) sealed multiple glazing units (j) lead (k) acrylic (l) polycarbonate (m) bullions		
4 Glass shop fronts	1 Component drawing reference	nr			D5 The component drawing referred to is to include details of the stiffeners		
				M4 Glass shop fronts involving simple glass joints and glass reinforcing fins are measured here. Suspended glass shop fronts are measured in Section H13			
5 Polished edges 6 Bevelled edges, width of bevel stated	1 Edges	m	1 Curved edges 2 Bent panes	M5 Labours on glass are grouped with the glass to which they relate		C2 Polished and bevelled edges are deemed to include external mitres	S6 Type and method of forming edges and shapings
	2 Internal mitres 3 Scallops and other shapings, details stated	nr		M6 Grinding, sandblasting and embossing are measured over the whole area of the pane			
7 Grinding 8 Sandblasting 9 Embossing	1 Plain work	m²	1 One or more dimensions ≤ 300 mm, size of pane stated				S 7 Type of acid work for embossing
10 Engraving	2 Design work	nr	1 Panes partly obscured 2 Panes wholly obscured 1 Dimensioned description				S8 Kind, quality and size of materials
11 Strips or channels for edges of panes		m	1 Fixed with other materials, type stated				

					S10 Method of fixing S11 Fixing through vulnerable materials
				...mirrors in toilets, dressing rooms and the like are measured in Section N10	M8 Hacking out existing glass and preparing rebates is measured the perimeter of the pane
		m	1 Beads for re-use, details stated		
13 Hacking out existing glass and preparing rebates	1 Type of sash or other surround and method of glazing stated together with type of glass				

L41 Lead light glazing

INFORMATION PROVIDED					MEASUREMENT RULES	DEFINITION RULES	COVERAGE RULES	SUPPLEMENTARY INFORMATION
P1 Information is shown on location drawings under A Preliminaries/General conditions								
CLASSIFICATION TABLE								
				1 Panes required to align with adjacent panes	M1 The requirement to state the average size of panes is related to each light			S1 Kind, quality and thickness of glass
1 Lead light glazing	1 Both dimensions of lights > 300 mm		1 Shape and average size of panes stated	m²					S2 Kind and quality of glazing compound
	2 One dimension only of lights ≤ 300 mm			m					S3 Method of glazing
	3 Both dimensions of lights ≤ 300 mm			nr					S4 Nature of frame or surround
2 Saddle bars	1 Length > 300 mm			m					S5 Type, section and nominal or finished width of cames and details of reinforcement
	2 Length ≤ 300 mm			nr					

INFORMATION PROVIDED		MEASUREMENT RULES	DEFINITION RULES	COVERAGE RULES	SUPPLEMENTARY INFORMATION
P1 Information is shown on location drawings under A Preliminaries/General conditions			D1 Work is deemed to be internal unless described as external		
CLASSIFICATION TABLE					
1 Infill panels (nr)	m²	1 Curved, radii stated 2 Panels, exceeding size of normal manufactured unit 3 Panels requiring special treatment to edges	D2 Infill panels are non-glass and non-glass plastics rigid sheet spandrel and infill panels of all kinds fixed with beads, gaskets and the like into wood, metal, plastics and concrete surrounds excluding panels/sheets forming an integral part of a component or proprietary cladding system	C1 Infill panels are deemed to include glazing compounds, sealants, intumescent mastic, distance pieces, location and setting blocks, and fixings	S1 Kind and quality of materials and if timber whether sawn or wrot S2 Preservative treatments applied as part of the production process S3 Surface treatments applied as part of the production process S4 Selection and protection for subsequent treatment S5 Matching grain or colour S6 Limits on planing margins on timber and if deviation from stated size is not permitted S7 Form of construction and jointing details where individual panel in more than one piece S8 Thickness or substance S9 Method of fixing where not at the discretion of the Contractor S10 Restrictions on cutting panels and treatment of edges

M Surface finishes

M10 Cement: sand/Concrete screeds/toppings

M12 Trowelled bitumen/resin/rubber-latex flooring

M13 Calcium sulfate based screeds

M20 Plastered/Rendered/Roughcast coatings

M23 Resin bound mineral coatings

J10 Specialist waterproof rendering

INFORMATION PROVIDED	MEASUREMENT RULES	DEFINITION RULES	COVERAGE RULES	SUPPLEMENTARY INFORMATION
P1 The following information is shown either on location drawings under A Preliminaries/General conditions or on further drawings which accompany the bills of quantities: (a) the scope and location of the work	M1 Resinous floor/wall finishes applied by brush or roller are measured in Section M60 M2 The area measured is that in contact with the base and no deduction is made for voids ≤ 0.50 m² or grounds M3 Work in staircase areas and plant rooms are each given separately M4 Work to ceilings and beams over 3.50 m above floor (measured to ceiling level in both cases), except in staircase areas, is so described stating the height in further 1.50 m stages M5 Curved work is so described with the radii stated measured on face	D1 The work is deemed internal unless described as external D2 The thickness stated is the nominal thickness D3 Rounded internal and external angles > 100 mm radius are classified as curved work D4 Floors include landings	C1 The work is deemed to include: (a) fair joints (b) outlets, working over and around obstructions, pipes and the like, into recesses and around shaped inserts (c) bonding agents where included with the work C2 Patterned work is deemed to include all extra work involved	S1 Kind, quality, composition and mix of materials including waterproofing agents and other admixtures and plasterboard or other rigid sheet lathing S2 Method of application S3 Nature of surface treatment including wax polishing or resin sealing coat S4 Special curing of finished work S5 Nature of base S6 Preparatory work where bonding is included with the work S7 Details of work to be carried out prior to fixing of frames or linings S8 Method of fixing and jointing plasterboard or other rigid sheet lathing

CLASSIFICATION TABLE

				DEFINITION RULES	COVERAGE RULES
1 Walls	1 Width > 300 mm		m²	1 Patterned, details stated	C3 Plasterboard or other sheet backing is deemed to include joint reinforcing scrim
2 Ceilings	2 Width ≤ 300 mm		m	2 Floors laid in bays, average size of bays stated	
3 Isolated beams	1 Thickness and number of coats stated			3 Floors laid in one operation with their base stated	C4 Work to walls, ceilings, beams and columns is deemed to include internal and external angles and
4 Isolated columns	2 Thickness of plasterboard or other rigid sheet lathing and thickness and number of coats stated			4 Overhand work	

D5 Work to sides and soffits of attached beams and openings and to sides of attached columns is classified as work to the abutting walls or ceilings

D6 Beams and columns are classified as isolated where

M6 Width is the width of each face

Item	Subdivision	Measurement / Dimension	Unit	Supplementary information	Rules
	2 To falls and crossfalls and to slopes ≤ 15° from horizontal 3 To slopes > 15° from horizontal				channels within the thickness of the screed or flooring (b) intersections in sloping work
7 Treads		1 Width and thickness stated	m	1 Patterned, details stated 2 Inserts, size or section stated 3 Moulded, shape stated	C6 Treads and risers are deemed to include fair edges, internal and external angles and intersections ≤ 10 mm radius
8 Risers	1 Plain 2 Undercut	1 Height and thickness stated 2 Dimensioned description	m		
9 Strings 10 Aprons		1 Width and thickness stated 2 Dimensioned description	m		C7 Strings and aprons are deemed to include ends, angles, ramped and wreathed corners and intersections ≤ 10 mm radius
11 Margins		1 Width and thickness stated 2 Dimensioned description	m		C8 Margins are deemed to include fair edges and flush joints
12 Linings to channels	1 Girth on face stated	1 Horizontal 2 To falls	m		C9 Linings to channels are deemed to include arrises, coves, ends, angles and intersections and outlets
13 Skirtings 14 Kerbs 15 Cappings		1 Height or width or girth and thickness stated 2 Dimensioned description	m	1 Patterned, details stated 2 Flush 3 Raking 4 Vertical 5 Inserts, size or section stated 6 Moulded, shape stated	C10 Skirtings, kerbs and cappings are deemed to include fair edges, rounded edges, beaded edges, coved junctions, ends, angles and ramps
16 Rounded angles and intersections			m		M7 Rounded angles and intersections are only measured in the range 10 – 100 mm radius

M10/M12/M13/M20/M23/J10 continued

CLASSIFICATION TABLE			Unit	MEASUREMENT RULES	DEFINITION RULES	COVERAGE RULES	SUPPLEMENTARY INFORMATION
17 Coves 18 Mouldings 19 Cornices 20 Architraves 21 Ceiling ribs		1 Girth stated 2 Dimensioned description --- 1 Patterned, details stated 2 Raking 3 Vertical 4 Enrichments 5 Undercut 6 Bracketing 7 Flat tops 8 Weathered tops	m	M8 Coves, mouldings, cornices, architraves, ceiling ribs and bands are measured the length in contact with the base			
	22 Bands 1 Flush 2 Raised 3 Sunk						
23 Items extra over the work in which they occur	1 Ends 2 Internal angles 3 External angles 4 Intersections	1 Details stated	nr	M9 Measured extra over 17 – 22.0.*.*			
24 Accessories	1 Reinforcement, details stated 2 Board insulation, thickness stated 3 Quilt insulation, thickness stated 4 Separating membranes, thickness stated	1 Walls 2 Ceilings 3 Isolated beams 4 Isolated columns 5 Floors 6 Roofs	m²				
	5 Movement joints 6 Cover strips 7 Dividing strip	1 Dimensioned description	m		D7 Movement joints include expansion joints		S9 Method of fixing where not at the discretion of the Contractor
	8 Beads, function stated 9 Nosings				D8 Function of beads as angle beads, casing beads, and the like are stated	C11 Beads and nosings are deemed to include working finishings thereto	
	10 Anti-crack strips ≤ 300 mm wide						
25 Precast plaster components	1 Dimensioned description		nr		D9 Components include vent grilles and ornaments		
26 Temporary support work to the face of risers and the like		1 Height stated 1 Undercut	m				

INFORMATION
S1 Proprietary name, kind, quality and thickness of board insulation and method of fixing
S2 Construction of metal lathing
S3 Kind, quality, composition, mix, and method of application and of materials for rendering
S4 Type of adhesive renders with glass fibre matting
S5 Nature of surface finish
S6 Nature of base
S7 Details of preparatory work where bonding is included with the work

C1 Work is deemed to include:
(a) fair joints
(b) working over and around obstructions into recesses and shaped inserts
(c) internal and external angles and intersections
(d) joint and reinforcing tape
(e) plaster dabs

C2 The work is deemed to include accessories for fixing

C3 Beads, nosings and expansion strips are deemed to include working finishings thereto

D1 The work is deemed external unless otherwise described as internal

D2 Rounded internal and external angles > 100 mm are classified as curved work

D3 The thickness stated is the nominal thickness

D4 Work to sides and soffits of openings is regarded as work to the abutting walls

D5 Function of beads as angle beads, casing beads, and the like are stated

M1 Only proprietary construction is measured in this Section

M2 Curved work is so described with the radii stated measured on face

M3 The area measured is that in contact with the base and no deduction is made for voids ≤ 0.50 m²

M4 Width is the width on face

P1 The following information is shown either on location drawings under A Preliminaries/General conditions or on further drawings:
(a) the scope and location of the work

CLASSIFICATION TABLE

1 Walls	1 Width > 300 mm	m²	1 Total thickness and number of coats of rendering stated	1 Overhand work
2 Ceilings	2 Width ≤ 300 mm	m		
3 Isolated beams				
4 Beads, function stated	1 Dimensioned description	m		
5 Nosings				
6 Expansion strips				

M22 Sprayed monolithic coatings

INFORMATION PROVIDED			MEASUREMENT RULES	DEFINITION RULES	COVERAGE RULES	SUPPLEMENTARY INFORMATION
P1 The following information is shown either on location drawings under A Preliminaries/General conditions or on further drawings which accompany the bills of quantities: (a) the scope and location of the work			M1 The area measured is that in contact with the base and no deduction is made for voids ≤ 0.50 m² or grounds M2 Work in staircase areas and plant rooms are each given separately M3 Work to ceilings and beams over 3.50 m above floor (measured to ceiling level in both cases), except in staircase areas, is so described stating the height in further 1.50 m stages	D1 The work is deemed internal unless described as external	C1 Work is deemed to include: (a) fair joints (b) additional labour for overhand work (c) angles, intersections and curved work	
CLASSIFICATION TABLE						S1 Kind and quantity of materials including plasterboard or other rigid sheet lathing S2 Nature of base S3 Preparatory work including bonding agents S4 Priming or sealing coats S5 Surface finish S6 Method of application
1 Walls and columns 2 Ceilings and beams 3 Structural metalwork	1 Thickness and number of coats stated 2 Thickness of plasterboard or other rigid sheet lathing and thickness and number of coats stated	m²				
4 Accessories	1 Beads, function stated 2 Nosings 3 Anti-crack strips ≤ 300 mm wide	m		D2 Function of beads as angle beads, casing beads, and the like are stated	C2 Beads and nosings are deemed to include working finishings thereto	S7 Method of fixing where not at the discretion of the Contractor

INFORMATION

S1 Kind and quality of materials

S2 Construction of framing and suspension system

S3 Extent of laps and method of jointing

C1 Work is deemed to include:
(a) mechanical fixings to solid backings, steel rods, stirrups, spacer rods and hangers
(b) steel channel framing
(c) screws, staples, clips, clout nails, wire ties, steel banding, and other fixings
(d) additional support and trimming for light fittings
(e) internal and external angles < 100 mm radius

C2 Bridging is deemed to include additional fixings

C3 Irregular window and cheeks are deemed to include cutting and extra supports

---

D1 All work is deemed internal unless described as external

D2 Rounded internal and external angles > 100 mm radius are classified as curved work

D3 Lathing to sides and soffits of attached beams and openings and to sides of attached columns is measured as work to the abutting walls or ceilings

D4 Lathing to ceilings includes lathing to sloping ceilings

M1 Work in staircase areas and plant rooms are each given separately

M2 Work to ceilings and beams over 3.50 m above floor (measured to ceiling level in both cases), except in staircase areas, is so described stating the height in further 1.50 m stages

M3 Curved work is so described with the radii stated measured on face

M4 The area measured is that between boundaries and no deduction is made for voids ≤ 0.50 m²

M5 Width is the width of each face

M6 Bridging is measured where the width of trunking or the like in the ceiling space obstructs the standard grid

---

P1 The following information is shown either on location drawings under A Preliminaries/General conditions or on further drawings which accompany the bills of quantities:
(a) the scope and location of the work
(b) the services located within the lathing, where the work includes complex integral services

CLASSIFICATION TABLE

Classification		Unit	Supplementary information	
1 Suspended lathing ceilings	1 Depth of suspension ≤ 150 mm 2 Depth of suspension 150–500 mm 3 and thereafter in 500 mm stages	m²	1 Method of fixing suspension system to structure	1 Suspension system obstructed by services
2 Walls	1 Width > 300 mm	m²	1 Method of fixing to structure	
3 Ceilings 4 Isolated beams 5 Isolated columns	2 Width ≤ 300 mm	m		
6 Upstands	1 Height ≤ 300 mm 2 and thereafter in 300 mm stages	m	1 Method of fixing suspension system to structure	
7 Bridging	1 Span stated	m	1 Supports to light fittings and the like	
8 Irregular window and dormer cheeks	1 Dimensioned description	nr		

M31 Fibrous plaster

	MEASUREMENT RULES	DEFINITION RULES	COVERAGE RULES	SUPPLEMENTARY INFORMATION
INFORMATION PROVIDED P1 The following information is shown either on location drawings under A Preliminaries/General conditions or on further drawings which accompany the bills of quantities: (a) the scope and location of the work	M1 Area measured is that in contact with the base and no deduction is made for voids ≤ 0.50 m² or grounds M2 Work in staircase areas and plant rooms are each given separately M3 Work to ceilings and beams over 3.50 m above floor (measured to ceiling level in both cases), except in staircase areas, is so described stating the height in further 1.50 m stages M4 Curved work is so described with the radii stated measured on face	D1 All work is deemed internal unless described as external	C1 Fibrous plaster is deemed to include: (a) fair joints (b) reinforcement (c) canvas (d) moulds (e) screws and other fixings	S1 Kind, quality, composition and mix of materials S2 Method of fixing and treatment of joints S3 Nature of base S4 Timber or metal lathing and reinforcement

CLASSIFICATION TABLE

					MEASUREMENT RULES	DEFINITION RULES	COVERAGE RULES
1 Walls	1 Width > 300 mm	1 Thickness stated		m²	M5 Width is the width of each face		
2 Ceilings	2 Width ≤ 300 mm			m			
3 Items extra over the fibrous plaster in which they occur	1 Access panels	1 Dimensioned description	1 Plain slab 2 Panelled slab 3 Patterned, details stated	nr			C2 Access panels are deemed to include cutting around edges and providing extra materials
4 Arches							
5 Domes							
6 Groined soffits							
7 Plain casings	1 Beams	1 Girth stated		m		D2 Plain casings to piers and pilasters are classified as to columns	
	2 Columns						
	3 Stanchions						
8 Moulded casings	1 Dimensioned description		1 Patterned, details stated 2 Shaft caps 3 Bases	nr			
9 Ornamental casings							

12 Cornices					their extreme lengths
13 Architraves				3 Vertical	
				4 Enrichments	
				5 Undercut	
14 Items extra over the work in which they occur	1 Ends 2 Internal angles 3 External angles 4 Intersections	1 Details stated	nr		M7 Measured extra over 10 – 13.0.1.*
15 Ornaments	1 Character stated	1 Dimensioned description	nr		D3 Ornaments are irregularly occuring features
16 Consoles					
17 Overdoors					
18 Canopies					
19 Fireplace surrounds					
20 Specially made models	1 Character stated			1 Temporarily fixed in the building for inspection 2 Modeller's grounds, details stated 3 Modeller's boards, details stated	
21 Full size cartoons					

110

M40 Stone/Concrete/Quarry/Ceramic tiling/Mosaic
M42 Wood block/Composition block/Parquet flooring

INFORMATION PROVIDED

P1 The following information is shown either on location drawings or on the bills of quantities which accompany the bills of quantities under A Preliminaries/General conditions or on further drawings
(a) the scope and location of the work

CLASSIFICATION TABLE

Item				Unit
1 Walls	1 Plain, width > 300 mm	1 Patterned, details stated		m²
	2 Plain, width ≤ 300 mm	2 Tiles with long side horizontal		m
	3 Work with joints laid out to detail, width > 300 mm	1 Dimensioned description		m²
	4 Work with joints laid out to detail, width ≤ 300 mm			m
2 Ceilings				
3 Isolated beams				
4 Isolated columns				
5 Floors	1 Level or to falls only ≤ 15° from horizontal	1 Plain	1 Patterned work, details stated	m²
	2 To falls and crossfalls and to slopes ≤ 15° from horizontal	2 Work with joints laid out to detail, dimensioned diagram stated	2 Floors laid in bays, average size of bays stated	
	3 To slopes > 15° from horizontal		3 Inserts, size or section stated	

MEASUREMENT RULES

M1 Work is measured on the exposed face and no deduction is made for voids ≤ 0.50 m²

M2 Work in staircase areas and plant rooms are each given separately

M3 Work to ceilings and beams over 3.50 m above floor (measured to ceiling level in both cases), except in staircase areas, is so described stating the height in further 1.50 m stages

M4 Curved work is so described with the radii stated measured on face

M5 Width is the width of each face

DEFINITION RULES

D1 All work is deemed internal unless described as external

D2 The thickness stated is the thickness exclusive of keys, grooves and the like

D3 Rounded internal and external angles > 10 mm radius are classified as curved work where not measured under 15.1–3.1.0

D4 Beams and columns are classified as isolated where the work is different from the abutting ceilings or walls

D5 Work to sides and soffits of attached beams and openings and to sides of attached columns is classed as work to the abutting walls or ceilings

D6 Tiles are deemed to be laid with their long side vertical unless otherwise described

D7 Floors include landings

COVERAGE RULES

C1 The work is deemed to include:
(a) fair joints
(b) working over and around obstructions
(c) additional labour for overhand work
(d) cutting
(e) drainage holes
(f) bedding mortars and adhesives
(g) grouting
(h) cleaning, sealing and polishing

C2 Work to walls, ceilings, beams and columns is deemed to include internal and external angles and intersections ≤ 10 mm radius

C3 Work to floors is deemed to include intersections in sloping work

SUPPLEMENTARY INFORMATION

S1 Kind and quality of materials
S2 Size, shape and thickness of units
S3 Nature of base
S4 Preparatory work
S5 Nature of finished surface including any sealing/polishing
S6 Bedding or other method of fixing
S7 Treatment of joints
S8 Layout of joints

Item	Classification	Unit	Supplementary information	Rules
8 Risers	1 Plain 2 Undercut	m	1 Height stated	C5 Curved treads, risers, strings and aprons are deemed to include curved and radiused cutting for special edge tiles
9 Strings 10 Aprons	1 Horizontal 2 To falls	m	1 Girth on face stated	C6 Strings and aprons are deemed to include fair edges, ends, angles and ramps
11 Linings to channels	1 Height stated	m		C7 Linings to channels are deemed to include arrises, coves, ends, angles, intersections and outlets
12 Skirtings 13 Kerbs	1 Height stated 2 Height and width stated	m	1 Patterned work, details stated 2 Inserts, size or section stated 3 Flush 4 Raking 5 Vertical	C8 Skirtings and kerbs are deemed to include fair edges, rounded edges, ends, angles and ramps
14 Corner pieces	1 Dimensioned description	nr		
15 Items extra over the work in which they occur	1 Special tiles 2 Special slabs 3 Special blocks	m	1 Dimensioned description 2 Manufacturer's reference	D8 Special tiles include non-standard tiles to produce fair edges, internal and external angles, moulded edges, beaded edges, and coved junctions
	4 Access units 5 Isolated special units	nr		
16 Accessories	1 Separating membranes, thickness stated	m²		
	2 Movement joints 3 Cover strips 4 Dividing strips	m	1 Dimensioned description	D9 Movement joints include expansion joints
	5 Ornaments, dimensioned description and character stated	nr	1 In situ 2 Precast 1 Undercut	D10 Ornaments are irregularly occurring features

S9 Method of fixing

M41 Terrazzo tiling/In situ terrazzo

INFORMATION PROVIDED	MEASUREMENT RULES	DEFINITION RULES	COVERAGE RULES	SUPPLEMENTARY INFORMATION
P1 The following information is shown either on location drawings under A Preliminaries/General conditions or on further drawings which accompany the bills of quantities: (a) the scope and location of the work				
CLASSIFICATION TABLE				
1 Terrazzo tiling	M1 Terrazzo tiling is measured in accordance with the rules for Section M40			
2 In situ terrazzo	M2 In situ terrazzo is measured in accordance with the rules for Section M10			

M50 Rubber/Plastics/Cork/Lino/Carpet tiling/sheeting
M51 Edge fixed carpeting

INFORMATION PROVIDED	MEASUREMENT RULES	DEFINITION RULES	COVERAGE RULES	SUPPLEMENTARY INFORMATION
P1 The following information is shown either on location drawings under A Preliminaries/General conditions or on further drawings which accompany the bills of quantities: (a) the scope and location of the work	M1 Area measured is that in contact with the base and no deduction is made for voids ≤ 0.50 m² M2 Work in staircase areas and plant rooms are each given separately M3 Work to ceilings and beams over 3.50 m above floor (measured to ceiling level in both cases), except in staircase areas, is so described stating the height in further 1.50 m stages	D1 The work is deemed internal unless described as external D2 Rounded internal and external angles > 100 mm radius are classified as curved work	C1 The work is deemed to include: (a) fair joints (b) working over and around obstructions, into recesses and shaped inserts (c) additional labour for overhand work (d) fixing at perimeter	S1 Kind, quality and size of materials S2 Nature and number of underlays S3 Extent of laps S4 Type of seams S5 Nature of base S6 Surface treatment S7 Pattern, width and laying direction of materials S8 Method of fixing and treatment of joints

			Unit			
3 Isolated beams						external angles ≤ 100 mm radius
4 Isolated columns				attached columns is classed as work to the abutting walls or ceilings		
5 Floors	1 Level or to falls only ≤ 15° from horizontal 2 To falls and crossfalls ≤ 15° from horizontal 3 To slopes > 15° from horizontal	3 Underlays		D4 Beams and columns are classified as isolated where the work is different from the abutting ceilings or walls respectively		C3 Work to floors is deemed to include working finishes, without necessity for cutting, into shallow channels C4 Work to falls, crossfalls and slopes is deemed to include intersections
6 Strings 7 Aprons 8 Treads	1 Width stated		m			C5 Work to strings and aprons is deemed to include ends, angles, ramped and weathered corners C6 Work to treads and risers is deemed to include all fair edges, internal and external angles
9 Risers	1 Plain 2 Undercut	1 Height stated	m			
10 Skirtings		1 Height stated	m		1 Patterned, details stated 2 Inserts, size or section stated 3 Flush 4 Raking 5 Vertical	C7 Work to skirtings and kerbs is deemed to include fair edges, rounded edges, beaded edges, moulded edges, coved junctions, ends, angles and ramps
11 Kerbs		2 Height and width stated				
12 Lining to channels		1 Girth on face stated	m		1 Patterned, details stated 2 Inserts, size or section stated	C8 Linings to channels are deemed to include arrises, coves, ends, angles, intersections and outlets
13 Accessories	1 Separating membranes, thickness stated	1 Dimensioned description	m^2			
	2 Nosings		m			C9 Nosings are deemed to include working finishings thereto C10 Mitred regular and irregular angles are deemed included
	3 Movement joints 4 Cover strips 5 Dividing strips			D5 Movement joints include expansion joints		
	6 Stair rods 7 Carpet holders 8 Carpet clips or grippers 9 Binder bars		nr	M6 Items are only measured separately where they are not fixings at perimeter see C1(d)		

M52 Decorative papers/fabrics

INFORMATION PROVIDED			MEASUREMENT RULES	DEFINITION RULES	COVERAGE RULES	SUPPLEMENTARY INFORMATION
P1 Information is shown on location drawings under A Preliminaries/General conditions			M1 Where the manufacturer and pattern cannot be fully described work is measured as hanging/fixing only and the supply and delivery to site of papers/fabrics is covered by a prime cost or provisional sum		C1 The work is deemed to include cutting or fitting around obstructions, intrusions or projections	S1 Kind and quality of materials, manufacturer and pattern
			M2 Work in staircase areas is given separately			S2 Nature of base
						S3 Preparatory work
			M3 The areas or lengths measured are the areas or lengths covered including allowances for the extra lengths of edges, mouldings, panels, sinkings, corrugations, flutings, carvings, enrichments and the like			S4 Method of fixing and jointing
			M4 No deduction is made for voids ≤ 0.50 m²			
			M5 Work to ceilings and beams over 3.50 m above floor (measured to ceiling level in both cases), except in staircase areas, is so described stating the height in further 1.50 m stages			

CLASSIFICATION TABLE

1 Walls and columns	1 Areas > 0.50 m²	m²	1 Raking and curved cutting	D1 Paper is deemed to be hung vertically unless described otherwise	
2 Ceilings and beams	2 Areas ≤ 0.50 m²	nr	2 Lining paper		
3 Border strips		m	1 Cutting border strips to profile		C2 Border strips are deemed to include mitres and intersections
4 Corners		nr	1 Cutting corners to profile		
5 Motifs			2 Cutting motifs to profile		

Y91 Off-site painting/Anti-corrosion treatments of common mechanical and/or electrical items

INFORMATION PROVIDED	MEASUREMENT RULES	DEFINITION RULES	COVERAGE RULES	SUPPLEMENTARY INFORMATION
P1 Information is shown on location drawings under A Preliminaries/General conditions	M1 Work in staircase areas and plant rooms are each given separately M2 The area or girth measured is the area or girth covered including allowances for the extra girth of edges, mouldings, panels, sinkings, corrugations, flutings, carvings, enrichments and the like unless otherwise provided herein. M3 No deduction is made for voids ≤ 0.50 m² M4 Work to ceilings and beams over 3.50 m above floor (measured to ceiling level in both cases), except in staircase areas, is so described stating the height in further 1.50 m stages	D1 Work is deemed to be internal unless otherwise described D2 Multi-coloured work is defined as the application of more than one colour on an individual surface except on walls and piers or on ceilings and beams D3 Multi-coloured work on walls and piers or on ceilings and beams shall be defined as the application in one room of more than one colour on either the walls and piers or ceilings and beams D4 Irregular surfaces are corrugated, fluted, panelled, carved or ornamental surfaces D5 Features unpainted include fire stripping and weather stripping D6 Isolated surfaces include the girth of associated mouldings D7 Where reference within this table is made to painting it is deemed to include clear finishing as applicable	C1 The work is deemed to include rubbing down with glass, emery or sand paper C2 Multi-coloured work is deemed to include cutting in and cutting to line	S1 Kind and quality of materials S2 Nature of base S3 Preparatory work S4 Priming or sealing coats (nr) S5 Undercoats (nr) S6 Finishing coats (nr) and surface finish S7 Method of application S8 Abrasive or other treatment applied between coats other than rubbing down with glass, emery or sand paper

CLASSIFICATION TABLE

1 General surfaces	1 Girth > 300 mm	m²	1 Multi-coloured work 2 Features unpainted, details stated 3 Irregular surfaces 4 Application on site prior to fixing 5 Application off-site prior to fixing
	2 Isolated surfaces, girth ≤ 300 mm	m	
	3 Isolated areas ≤ 0.50 m² irrespective of girth	nr	

D8 General surfaces are those not included in other Classifications

C3 Work to general surfaces is deemed to include work on butts and fastenings attached to doors, frames and linings

M60/M61/Y91 continued

CLASSIFICATION TABLE			Unit		MEASUREMENT RULES	DEFINITION RULES	COVERAGE RULES	SUPPLEMENTARY INFORMATION
2 Glazed windows and screens	1 Panes, area ≤ 0.10 m²	1 Girth > 300 mm	m²	1 Multi-coloured work	M5 The area measured is each side of windows, screens and glazed doors, measured flat plus edges of glazed doors	D9 Pane areas are those of individual panes	C4 Glazed work is deemed to include: (a) edges of opening lights and portions uncovered by sliding sashes in double hung casements (b) additional painting to the surrounding frame caused by opening lights (c) cutting in next glass (d) work on glazing beads, butts and fastenings attached thereto	
3 Glazed sash windows	2 Panes, area 0.10 – 0.50 m²	2 Isolated surfaces, girth ≤ 300 mm	m	2 Features unpainted, details stated				
4 Glazed doors	3 Panes, area 0.50 – 1.00 m²	3 Isolated areas ≤ 0.50 m² irrespective of girth	nr	3 Partially glazed	M6 Where panes of more than one size occur then the sizes are averaged			
	4 Panes, area > 1.00 m²			4 Irregular surfaces	M7 Work to associated linings and sills are measured as general surfaces			
				5 Application on site to members prior to fixing				
				6 Application off site to members prior to fixing				
5 Structural metalwork	1 General surfaces	1 Girth > 300 mm	m²	1 Multi-coloured work	M8 The height of structural metalwork is measured to the highest point of the members in the stated height range		C5 Work to structural metalwork is deemed to include work to attached hookbolts, clips and the like	
	2 Members of roof trusses, lattice girders, purlins and the like	2 Isolated surfaces, girth ≤ 300 mm	m	2 Features unpainted, details stated				
		3 Isolated areas ≤ 0.50 m² irrespective of girth	nr	3 Application on site to members prior to fixing				
				4 Application off site to members prior to fixing				
				5 Structural metalwork height 5.00 – 8.00 m above floor level				
				6 and thereafter in 3.0 m stages				
6 Radiators	1 Panel type	1 Girth > 300 mm	m²		M9 Radiators are measured the area painted		C6 Work to radiators is deemed to include work to brackets and stays	
	2 Column type	2 Isolated surfaces, girth ≤ 300 mm	m					
		3 Isolated areas ≤ 0.50 m² irrespective of girth	nr					
7 Railings, fences and gates	1 Plain open type	1 Girth > 300 mm	m²		M10 Plain open type fencing and gates are classified according to the size of their individual members	D10 Examples of plain open type fencing are plain post and wire, post and rail, chain link, wire mesh, cleft pale, palisade and metal bar		
		2 Isolated surfaces, girth ≤ 300 mm	m		M11 Each side of close type fencing and gates is measured overall	D11 Examples of close type fencing are close boarded, built up concrete and corrugated		
		3 Isolated areas ≤ 0.50 m² irrespective of girth	nr					
	2 Close type		m²		M12 Each side of ornamental railings and gates is measured and notwithstanding the general measurement rule above is measured overall regardless of voids			
	3 Ornamental type							

		2 Isolated surfaces, girth ≤ 300 mm	m		
		3 Isolated areas ≤ 0.50 m² irrespective of girth	nr		
9 Services		1 Girth > 300 mm	m²	1 Multi-coloured work	D12 Services include pipes, lagged pipes, conduits, cables, ducting, trunking, straps, standards, bars and the like
		2 Isolated surfaces, girth ≤ 300 mm	m	2 Features unpainted, details stated	
		3 Isolated areas ≤ 0.50 m² irrespective of girth	nr	3 Painted throughout in coded colours	D13 Painting to isolated services units such as ventilating gratings, soot-doors, flushing cisterns, rainwater heads, strap hinges and the like is classed as painting services
				4 Application on site to members prior to fixing	
				5 Application off site prior to fixing	
10 Coloured bands for coding service pipes	1 Colours (nr)	1 Description stated	nr		

C8 Work to services is deemed to include work to saddles, pipehooks, holderbats, conduit boxes and other components for fixing

N Furniture/Equipment

N10 General fixtures/furnishings/equipment
N11 Domestic kitchen fittings
N12 Catering equipment
N13 Sanitary appliances/fittings
N15 Signs/Notices
N20, 21, 22, 23 Special purpose fixtures/furnishings/equipment
Q50 Site/Street furniture/equipment

INFORMATION PROVIDED				MEASUREMENT RULES	DEFINITION RULES	COVERAGE RULES	SUPPLEMENTARY INFORMATION
P1 Information is shown on location drawings under A Preliminaries/General conditions				M1 It is permissible in respect of any individual item to use any other appropriate Rule in this document provided that it is stated which Rules have been applied to which item	D1 Fixtures, furnishings, equipment, fittings and appliances consist of those items listed as Sections N10 – 13, N15, N20 – 23 and Q50 at Appendix A excluding signwriting and carving and sculpting		S1 Such information as is appropriate to the procurement, design, execution, supply and/or manufacture of the item and its incorporation in the Works
CLASSIFICATION TABLE							S2 Details of excavation and concrete backfilling for foundations to Site/Street furniture/equipment
1 Fixtures, furnishings and equipment not associated with services	1 Component drawing reference		nr				S3 Specified codes of practice and regulations
	2 Dimensioned diagram						S4 Kind and quality of materials
2 Signwriting	1 Dimensioned description						S5 Gauge, thickness or substance of materials
3 Carving and sculpting							S6 Tests with which
4 Fittings, equipment and appliances associated with services	1 Type, size and pattern, capacity, loading as appropriate and method of fixing all stated	1 Cross reference to specification	nr	1 Ancillaries provided with fittings, equipment and appliances, details stated		C1 Providing everything necessary for jointing is deemed to be included	
				2 Integral controls and indicators stated			
				3 Remote controls and indicators and connections between, details stated			
				M2 Marking positions, loose ancillaries, identification, testing and commissioning, temporary operation, preparing drawings, operating and maintenance manuals are measured in Sections Y51, Y54 and Y59 as appropriate			

			...treatments applied off site stating whether applied before or after fabricating or assembly S9 Limiting dimensions on the size and weight of equipment		
			appliances, details stated 5 Initial charges, details stated 6 Method of fixing and background stated	1 Integral controls or indicators stated 2 Remote controls or indicators and connections between. details stated	C2 Jointing ancillaries to fittings. equipment or appliances is deemed to be included
5 Ancillaries not provided with the fittings. equipment or appliances	1 Type, size and method of jointing stated	nr	1 Type of fitting, equipment or appliance stated		
6 Fixtures. furnishings. equipment. fittings and appliances provided by the Employer	1 Type, size and method of fixing stated	nr	1 Provision of additional components. details stated 2 Background stated		C3 Accepting delivery, storing and handling are deemed to be included

P Building fabric sundries

P10 Sundry insulation/proofing work/fire stops

INFORMATION PROVIDED		MEASUREMENT RULES	DEFINITION RULES	COVERAGE RULES	SUPPLEMENTARY INFORMATION
P1 Information is shown on location drawings under A Preliminaries/General conditions			D1 Sundry insulation/proofing work/fire stops include: (a) flexible sheets, insulating boards and other materials, where not specified as part of another section, laid, hung or fixed horizontally, sloping or vertically as waterproofing, vapour barriers, fire stops, fire barriers, isolating membranes, sound insulation or thermal insulation (b) mineral fibre, plastics bead and cellulose loose fill thermal insulation laid between joists, etc.		
		M1 The area measured is that covered M2 Proofing work/fire stops are only measured independently in this Section where not specified as part of another Work Section	D2 Horizontal includes the upper surface of any sloping structure ≤ 45° from the horizontal D3 Vertical includes the upper surface of any sloping structure > 45° from the horizontal D4 Soffit includes the underside of any horizontal or sloping structure	C1 All cutting is deemed to be included	S1 Type, quality and thickness of material S2 Extent of laps S3 Method of fixing where not at the discretion of the Contractor

CLASSIFICATION TABLE

1 Sheets 2 Quilts 3 Boards 4 Loose fill	1 Plain areas 2 Across members, centres of members stated 3 Between members, centres of members stated	1 Horizontal 2 Vertical 3 Soffit	m²

					INFORMATION
P1 Information is shown on location drawings under A Preliminaries/General conditions					

CLASSIFICATION TABLE

1 Filling	1 Thickness stated	m²	M1 The area measured is that filled	D1 Foamed/Fibre/Bead cavity wall insulation includes foamed resin or loose fill insulation injected or blown into cavity walls	S1 Type and quality of material S2 Method of application including associated works

P20 Unframed isolated trims/skirtings/sundry items

INFORMATION PROVIDED			MEASUREMENT RULES	DEFINITION RULES	COVERAGE RULES	SUPPLEMENTARY INFORMATION
P1 Information is shown on location drawings under A Preliminaries/General conditions			M1 Items which do not have a constant cross-section are so described and given stating the extreme dimensions M2 Items are only measured independently in this Section where not specified as part of another Work Section M3 Curved work is so described with the radii stated	D1 All timber sizes are nominal sizes unless stated as finished sizes	C1 The work is deemed to include ends, angles, mitres, intersections and the like except on hardwood items > 0.003 m² sectional area	

CLASSIFICATION TABLE

			MEASUREMENT RULES			SUPPLEMENTARY INFORMATION
1 Skirtings, picture rails, architraves and the like 2 Cover fillets, stops, trims, beads, nosings and the like 3 Isolated shelves and worktops 4 Window boards 5 Unframed pinboards 6 Duct covers 7 Isolated handrails and grab rails	1 Dimensioned overall cross-section description	m	1 Built up timber members, size of components stated 2 Timber components tongued on 3 Different cross-section shapes (nr) 4 Stopped labours (nr)	M4 Associated handrails are measured in Section L30		S1 Kind and quality of materials and if timber whether sawn or wrot S2 Preservative treatments applied as part of the production process S3 Surface treatments applied as part of the production process S4 Selection and protection for subsequent treatment S5 Matching grain or colour S6 Limits on planing margins on timber and if deviation from stated size is not permitted S7 Method of jointing or form of construction S8 Method of fixing where not at the discretion of the Contractor S9 Fixing through vulnerable materials
8 Extra over the hardwood items, > 0.003 m² sectional area, in which they occur	1 Ends 2 Angles 3 Mitres 4 Intersections	nr				
9 Backboards, plinth blocks and the like	1 Dimensioned description	nr	1 Built up timber members, size of components stated 2 Timber components tongued on 3 Stopped labours (nr)			

P1 Information is shown on location drawings under A Preliminaries/General conditions

CLASSIFICATION TABLE

1 Type of item, unit or set stated	1 Nature of base stated			
		nr		

D1 Ironmongery consists of the items listed as Section P21 at Appendix A of these rules

C1 Ironmongery is deemed to include fixing with screws to match and preparing base to receive same

S1 Kind and quality of materials and fixings

S2 Surface finish

S3 Constituent parts of the units or sets

S4 Fixing through vulnerable materials

P22 Sealant joints

INFORMATION PROVIDED	MEASUREMENT RULES	DEFINITION RULES	COVERAGE RULES	SUPPLEMENTARY INFORMATION
P1 The following information is shown on location drawings under A Preliminaries/General conditions or on further drawings which accompany the bills of quantities (a) scope and location of the work		D1 Sealant joints include forming sealant joints which for special reasons cannot reasonably be included in another Work Section as follows: (a) general expansion joints in the building not associated with any particular type of work (b) sealant joints required to be executed by a sealant specialist (c) renewal of sealant joints in existing buildings where not associated with replacement or refixing of a component		
	M1 Lengths are measured on face	D2 Vertical joints include work inclined ≤ 10° from vertical D3 Sloping joints include work to upper surfaces inclined > 10° from horizontal and > 10° from vertical D4 Soffit joints include all inclined soffits D5 Horizontal joints include work inclined ≤ 10° from horizontal	C1 Work is deemed to include preparation, cleaners, primers and sealers appropriate to the contact surface C2 Raking out existing materials is deemed to include raking out/cutting back the existing components sufficiently to accommodate the new system, disposal, and any make up filler where excess is removed	S1 Kind and quality of materials S2 Method of application S3 Preparation of contact surfaces, cleaners, primers and sealers

CLASSIFICATION TABLE

1 Joints, contact surfaces stated	1 Vertical 2 Sloping 3 Soffit 4 Horizontal	m	1 Raking out existing materials
2 Pointing, contact surfaces stated		m	

P30 Trenches/Pipeways/Pits for buried engineering services
P31 Holes/Chases/Covers/Supports for services

			MEASUREMENT RULES	DEFINITION RULES	COVERAGE RULES	SUPPLEMENTARY INFORMATION
INFORMATION PROVIDED						S1 Kind and quality of materials
P1 Information regarding the nature of excavation work is described in accordance with Section D20, Information Provided			M1 Unless identified in these sections all other items of Builder's work associated with plumbing, mechanical and electrical installations are given in accordance with the appropriate Work Sections			
P2 The following information is shown either on location drawings under A Preliminaries/General conditions or on further drawings which accompany the bills of quantities:						
(a) the layout of the services			M2 Builder's work in connection with plumbing, mechanical and electrical installations are each identified under an appropriate heading			
CLASSIFICATION TABLE						
1 Excavating trenches	1 Services ≤ 200 mm nominal size	1 Commencing level stated where > 0.25 m below existing ground level	m	M3 Special materials for backfilling are stated in accordance with Section D20:9.*.*.*	D1 Trenches next to roadways, next to existing buildings, and in unstable ground are defined in accordance with D20:7.*.*.3 – 5	C1 Excavating trenches are deemed to include:	S2 Specified protection where required
	2 Services > 200 mm nominal size, nominal size stated	2 Curved				(a) earthwork support	
		2 and therafter in 250 mm stages		M4 Surface treatments are stated in accordance with D20:13.*.*.*		(b) consolidation of trench bottoms	
		3 Below ground water level				(c) trimming excavations	
		4 Next to roadways		M5 Excavating trenches below ground water level is measured where the ground water level is above the bottom of the trench	D2 Backfilling with special materials occurs where selected or treated excavated materials, or imported materials are used	(d) special protection of services	
		5 Next to existing buildings				(e) backfilling with and compaction of excavated materials	
		6 Unstable ground				(f) disposal of surplus excavated materials	
		7 Specified multiple handling details stated			D3 Active, toxic/hazardous materials as defined Section D20 Rules D2 and D3		
		8 Disposal at specified locations, details stated					
		9 Backfilling with special materials, details stated					
		10 Surface treatment, details stated					
		11 Active material					
		12 Toxic/hazardous material, type stated					

P30/P31 continued

CLASSIFICATION TABLE		Unit			MEASUREMENT RULES	DEFINITION RULES	COVERAGE RULES	SUPPLEMENTARY INFORMATION
2 Items extra over excavating trenches, irrespective of depth	1 Breaking out existing materials	m³	1 Rock 2 Concrete		M6 The measurement of extra over items is based on the width of the beds in the trenches. Where there are no beds the width to be taken is the nominal size of the service plus 300 mm. In both cases measurement is subject to a minimum width of 500 mm	D4 **Rock is any material which is of such size or position that it can only be removed by wedges, special plant or explosives**		
	2 Breaking out existing hard pavings, thickness stated	m²	3 Reinforced concrete 4 Brickwork, blockwork or stonework 5 Coated macadam or asphalt	1 Reinstating to match existing				
	3 Lifting turf for preservation		1 Method of preserving, details stated					
	4 Next existing live services	m	1 Type and number of services stated		M7 To be measured where precautions are specifically required			S3 Nature of special requirement
	5 Around existing live services crossing trench	nr						
3 Disposal	1 Surface water	item				D5 Surface water is water on the surface of the site and the excavations		
	2 Ground water				M8 An item for disposal of ground water is only measured where a corresponding item is measured in accordance with 1.*.*.3 and is adjusted accordingly if the post contract water level is different			
4 Beds		m	1 Width and thickness of bed stated					
5 Beds and haunchings			1 Nominal size of service stated				C2 Beds, haunchings, surrounds and casings are deemed to include formwork	
6 Beds and surrounds			1 Width, thickness of bed and thickness of surround stated					
7 Vertical casings			1 Size stated					
8 Stop cock pits, valve chambers and the like		nr	1 Type, size and method of construction stated					
9 Other chambers					M9 Other chambers are measured in accordance with the Section R12 rules for manholes			

			Unit			Rules
11 Items extra over the duct in which they occur	3 Flexible 1 Fittings 2 Special treatment at ends	1 Description and method of jointing stated	nr			
12 Cover tiles 13 Identification tapes	1 Straight 2 Curved, radii stated	1 Type and size stated	m	1 Use of special colours for differing services 2 Staged laying 3 Handed to others for laying		
14 Marker posts 15 Marker plates	1 Type and size stated	1 Setting in hole, concrete or other material 2 Fixing to walls or other surfaces 3 Handed to others for setting or fixing	nr	1 Lettering required		
16 Surface boxes 17 Access chambers 18 Inspection chambers	1 Type, size and covers stated	1 Bedding, and jointing, details stated 2 Handed to others for fixing	nr			
19 Cutting or forming holes, mortices, sinkings and chases for electrical installations	1 Concealed conduits, type stated 2 Concealed cables, type stated 3 Exposed conduits, type stated 4 Exposed cables, type stated	1 Luminaire points 2 Socket outlet points 3 Fitting outlet points 4 Equipment and control gear points 5 Any point in unusually expensive coverings	nr	1 Making good 2 Making good vulnerable materials, details stated	M10 Points are enumerated irrespective of size, type and kind	C3 Associated switch points are deemed to be included
20 Cutting or forming holes for other services installations	1 Ducts, nature and thickness of structure stated	1 Girth ≤ 1.00 m 2 Girth 1.00 – 2.00 m 3 and therafter in 1.00 m stages	nr	1 Rectangular 2 Circular 3 Dimensioned profile and description 4 Making good		D6 Ducts include trays, trunking, gratings and the like
	2 Pipes, nature and thickness of structure stated	1 ≤ 55 mm nominal size 2 55-110 mm nominal size 3 > 110 mm nominal size				D7 Pipes include tubes, bars, cables, conduit and the like

P30/P31 continued

CLASSIFICATION TABLE				Unit		MEASUREMENT RULES	DEFINITION RULES	COVERAGE RULES	SUPPLEMENTARY INFORMATION
21 Cutting or forming mortices, sinkings and the like for other services installations	1 Size stated	1 Nature of structure stated	1 Making good	nr					
22 Cutting or forming chases for other services installations	1 Number and size of services stated				m				
23 Pipe and duct sleeves	1 Building in 2 Other fixing	1 Type, size of pipe or duct and nature of structure stated	1 Fix only 2 Bedding and pointing 3 Fire resistant packing 4 Water proofing 5 Making good 6 Method of fixing stated	nr					
24 Ends of supports for services equipment, fittings, appliances and ancillaries	1 Type and size of support stated		1 Fix only 2 Bedding and pointing 3 Making good 4 Method of fixing and background stated	nr					
25 Ends of supports for pipes and ducts	1 Pipes and ducts ≤ 55 mm nominal size	1 Grouped together stating spacing of supports		m		M11 Measured net length of pipe or duct over all fittings			
	2 Pipes and ducts > 55 mm nominal size	2 Size and type of pipe or duct stated		nr					
26 Special measures where services pass through walls, floors, ceilings and roofs	1 Type of measure and size stated	1 Method of fixing and nature of structure stated		nr			D8 Special measures include precautions against the spread of fire and water		
27 Trench covers and frames	1 Type and width stated	1 Method of fixing and background stated	1 Limitations to length of covers stated	m					
28 Duct covers and frames									
29 Blockings, grounds and fixings for services	1 Type and size stated	1 Method of fixing and nature of structure stated		nr					

					M12 Measured net, no allowance for sag	
3 Wall and soffit brackets and hangers						
4 Pole brackets						
5 Stays						
6 Proprietary support components						
31 Catenary cables	1 Type and size stated	m	1 Method of fixing and background stated	1 Eye bolts, details stated 2 Shackles, details stated 3 Straining screws, details stated		

Work to existing buildings

					M13 Cutting holes for services installations and making good after is measured in accordance with the appropriate Work Sections	
32 Cutting mortices and sinkings for services installations	1 Size stated	nr	1 Nature of structure stated			
33 Cutting chases for services installations	1 Number and size of services stated	m				
34 Lifting and replacing floor boards	1 For pipes or ducts	1 Number and nominal size of pipe or duct stated	m	1 Making good, details stated	M14 No distinction is made between routes parallel to or at an angle to the floor boards	C4 Cutting floor boards and notching or holing joists are deemed to be included
	2 For cables or conduits	2 ≤ 3 cables or conduits 3 3 – 6 cables or conduits 4 > 6 cables or conduits				
35 Lifting and replacing chequer plates, trench covers and duct covers	1 Type and width stated	m				

Q Paving/Planting/Fencing/Site furniture

Q10 Kerbs/Edgings/Channels/Paving accessories

INFORMATION PROVIDED				MEASUREMENT RULES	DEFINITION RULES	COVERAGE RULES	SUPPLEMENTARY INFORMATION
P1 The following information is shown either on location drawings under A Preliminaries/General conditions or on further drawings which accompany the bills of quantities: (a) the scope and location of the work				M1 In situ concrete kerbs/edgings/channels to in situ concrete roads are measured in Section Q21			
CLASSIFICATION TABLE							
1 Excavation				M2 Excavation work is measured in accordance with Section D20			
2 Kerbs 3 Edgings 4 Channels		m	1 Dimensioned description	1 Sizes and extent of reinforcement 2 Foundation and haunching 3 Curved, radii stated	M3 Where otherwise identical units are required which vary in their length, the number of units is to be stated in the item	C1 Kerbs, edgings and channels are deemed to include cut angles and ends C2 Foundation and haunching is deemed to include formwork	S1 Kind and quality of materials S2 Mix details S3 Bedding and fixings S4 Surface finishes S5 Nature and extent of foundation and haunching
5 Items extra over the work in which they occur		nr	1 Specials				
6 Paving accessories			1 Dimension description				

INFORMATION PROVIDED	MEASUREMENT RULES	DEFINITION RULES	COVERAGE RULES	SUPPLEMENTARY INFORMATION
P1 The following information is shown either on location drawings under A Preliminaries/General conditions or on further drawings which accompany the bills of quantities: (a) the scope and location of the work				
CLASSIFICATION TABLE				
1 Concrete	M1 Concrete is measured in accordance with Section E10			
2 Formwork	M2 Formwork is measured in accordance with Section E20			
3 Reinforcement	M3 Reinforcement is measured in accordance with Section E30			
4 Joints	M4 Joints are measured in accordance with Section E40			
5 Worked finishes	M5 Worked finishes are measured in accordance with Section E41			
6 Accessories cast in	M6 Accessories cast in are measured in accordance with Section E42			

Q22 Coated macadam/Asphalt roads/pavings

INFORMATION PROVIDED		MEASUREMENT RULES	DEFINITION RULES	COVERAGE RULES	SUPPLEMENTARY INFORMATION
P1 The following information is shown either on location drawings under A Preliminaries/General conditions or on further drawings which accompany the bills of quantities: (a) the scope and location of the work			D1 Work is deemed external unless described as internal D2 The thickness stated is the finished thickness	C1 Work is deemed to include: (a) fair joints (b) working over and around obstructions into recesses and shaped inserts	S1 Kind, composition and mix of materials S2 Method of application S3 Nature of surface treatment S4 Special curing of finished work S5 Nature of base S6 Preparatory work where bonding is included with the finish
CLASSIFICATION TABLE					
1 Roads 2 Pavings	1 Thickness and number of coats stated	1 Level and to falls only 2 To falls and crossfalls and to slopes ≤ 15° from horizontal 3 To slopes > 15° from the horizontal	m²	M1 The area measured is that in contact with the base and no deduction is made for voids ≤ 0.50 m² or grounds	C2 Work is deemed to include forming or working into shallow channels and associated labours C3 Work to falls and crossfalls, and to slopes is deemed to include intersections
3 Linings to channels	1 Horizontal 2 To falls	1 Girth on face stated	m		C4 Linings to channels are deemed to include arrises, coves, ends, angles, intersections and outlets

				INFORMATION
P1 The following information is shown either on location drawings under A Preliminaries/General conditions or on further drawings which accompany the bills of quantities: (a) the scope and location of the work				S1 Kind and quality of materials

CLASSIFICATION TABLE

1 Roads 2 Pavings	1 Thickness stated	1 Level and to falls only 2 To falls and crossfalls and to slopes ≤ 15° from horizontal 3 To slopes > 15° from horizontal	m²	M1 Area measured is that in contact with base and no deduction is made for voids ≤ 0.50 m²	D1 Work is deemed external unless described as internal D2 The thickness stated is the compacted thickness	C1 The work is deemed to include: (a) fair joints (b) working over and around obstructions into recesses and shaped inserts	S2 Formation, preparation and surface finish or treatment S3 Laying and compaction
3 Edgings	1 Thickness and height stated		m			C2 Edgings are deemed to include: (a) pegs and supports (b) angles and ends	S4 Type and method of fixing or support

Q24 Interlocking brick/block roads/pavings
Q25 Slab/Brick/Block/Sett/Cobble pavings

INFORMATION PROVIDED			MEASUREMENT RULES	DEFINITION RULES	COVERAGE RULES	SUPPLEMENTARY INFORMATION
P1 The following information is shown either on location drawings under A Preliminaries/General conditions or on further drawings which accompany the bills of quantities: (a) the scope and location of the work				D1 Work is deemed external unless otherwise described D2 The thickness stated is the nominal thickness	C1 Work is deemed to include: (a) fair joints (b) working over and around obstructions into recesses and shaped inserts (c) cutting	S1 Kind and quality of materials including bedding S2 Size, shape and thickness of units S3 Nature of surface finish S4 Bedding or other method of fixing S5 Treatment of joints S6 Layout of joints S7 Nature of base S8 Preparatory work
CLASSIFICATION TABLE						
1 Roads 2 Pavings	1 Thickness stated	m²	1 Level and to falls only 2 To falls and crossfalls and to slopes ≤ 15° from the horizontal 3 To slopes > 15° from the horizontal	M1 Work is measured on the exposed face and no deduction is made for voids ≤ 0.50 m²		C2 Work is deemed to include forming or working finishes into shallow channels including all associated labours C3 Work to falls and crossfalls and to slopes ≤ 15° is deemed to include all intersections	
			1 Bedding, thickness stated 2 Patterned, details stated 3 Work with joints laid out to detail, components detail drawing reference stated 4 Laid in bays, average size of bays stated			
3 Treads 4 Margins	1 Width stated	m	1 Patterned, details stated 2 Foundation and haunching 3 Curved, radii stated			C4 Work is deemed to include all fair edges, internal and external angles C5 Linings to channels are deemed to include edges, angles, intersections and outlets C6 Foundation and haunching is deemed to include formwork	S9 Nature and extent of foundation and haunching
5 Risers	1 Height stated					
6 Kerbs 7 Edgings	1 Dimensioned description			M2 Kerbs, edgings and channels in a similar material to the roads/pavings are measured here. Independent kerbs, edgings and channels are measured in Section Q10		
8 Linings to channels	1 Girth on face stated					
9 Items extra over the work in which they occur	1 Dimensioned description	m				
	2 Isolated special units	nr				
10 Accessories	1 Separating membranes	m²	1 Thickness stated			
	2 Movement joints	m	1 Dimensioned description 1 Curved, radii stated		D4 Movement joints include	

INFORMATION

S1 Kind and quality of materials
S2 Nature of base

S3 Number of coats
S4 Surface finish
S5 Method of application

S6 Methods of fixing and treatment of joints
S7 Extent of laps
S8 Type of seams

S9 Proprietary name
S10 Method of application
S11 Surface treatment

S12 Preparatory work
S13 Coats (nr)
S14 Method of application
S15 Treatment applied between coats

C1 Work is deemed to include:
(a) fair joints
(b) working over and around obstructions into recesses and shaped inserts
(c) cutting

C2 Work is deemed to include forming or working into shallow channels and associated labours

C3 Work to falls and crossfalls and slopes is deemed to include intersections

---

D1 Work is deemed external unless described as internal
D2 The thickness stated is the nominal thickness

M1 The area measured is that in contact with the base and no deduction is made for voids $\leq 0.50\ m^2$

P1 The following information is shown either on location drawings under A Preliminaries/General conditions or on further drawings which accompany the bills of quantities:
(a) the scope and location of the work

CLASSIFICATION TABLE

			Unit
1 Liquid applied surfacings	1 Level and to falls only		m²
	2 To falls and crossfalls and to slopes ≤ 15° from the horizontal		
	3 To slopes > 15° from the horizontal		
2 Sheet surfacings	1 Thickness stated		
3 Tufted surfacings			
4 Proprietary coloured tarmacadam sports surfacings and pavings	1 Thickness and number of coats stated		
5 Proprietary clay and shale coloured sports surfacings and pavings			
6 Proprietary no fines concrete sports surfacings and pavings	1 Thickness stated		
7 Surface dressings			
8 Line marking	1 Width ≤ 300 mm		m
	2 Width > 300 mm, width stated		
9 Letters and figures	1 Dimensioned description		nr

Q30 Seeding/Turfing

INFORMATION PROVIDED			MEASUREMENT RULES	DEFINITION RULES	COVERAGE RULES	SUPPLEMENTARY INFORMATION
P1 The following information is shown either on location drawings under A Preliminaries/General conditions or on further drawings which accompany the bills of quantities: (a) the scope and location of the work						

CLASSIFICATION TABLE

			MEASUREMENT RULES	DEFINITION RULES	COVERAGE RULES	SUPPLEMENTARY INFORMATION
1 Cultivating	1 Depth stated	m²		D1 Types of surface applications include herbicides, selective weedkillers, peat, manure, compost, mulch, fertilizer, soil ameliorants, sand and the like	C1 Cultivating is deemed to include the removal of stones	S1 Timing of operations
2 Surface applications	1 Type and rate stated				C2 Surface applications are deemed to include working in if required	S2 Method of cultivating and degree of tilth
3 Seeding	1 Rate stated				C3 Seeding is deemed to include raking or harrowing in and rolling	S3 Kind, quality, composition and mix of materials
4 Turfing					C4 Cutting is deemed to include edge trimming	S4 Method of application
5 Turfing edges of seeded areas	1 Width stated					S5 Method of securing turves
6 Protection	1 Temporary fencing	m	M1 Protective temporary fencing is only measured here where specifically required and then in accordance with Section Q40			
	1 Duration and ultimate ownership, details stated					
7. Maintenance	1. Details stated	Item				

Q31 External planting
Q32 Internal planting

INFORMATION PROVIDED		MEASUREMENT RULES	DEFINITION RULES	COVERAGE RULES	SUPPLEMENTARY INFORMATION
P1 The following information is shown either on location drawings under A Preliminaries/General conditions or on further drawings which accompany the bills of quantities: (a) the scope and location of the work					

Item	First subdivision	Second subdivision	Unit	Supplementary
1 Cultivating	1 Depth stated		m²	1 Weeding, details stated
				2 Fallowing, details stated
2 Surface applications	1 Type and rate stated			
3 Trees	1 Botanical name	1 BS size designation and root system stated	nr	1 Planting in cultivated or grassed areas prepared by others, details stated
		2 Girth, height and clear stem and root system stated		2 Indoor planting, details stated
				3 Initial cut back, details stated
				4 Supports and ties
				5 Refilling with special materials, details stated
				6 Watering, details stated
4 Young nursery stock trees	1 Height and root system stated		nr	
5 Shrubs				
6 Hedge plants	1 Height stated		nr	
	2 Height, spacing, number of rows, and layout stated		m	
7 Herbaceous plants	1 Size stated		nr	
	2 Size and number per m² stated		m²	
8 Bulbs, corms and tubers	1 Size stated		nr / kg	
9 Mulching after planting	1 Around individual plants	1 Thickness and area stated	nr	1 Tree spats, details stated
	2 Beds	2 Thickness stated	m²	
10 Protection	1 Tree guards	1 Dimensioned description	nr	
	2 Anti-desiccant sprays	2 Height and girth of tree or spread of plant stated		
	3 Wrapping	3 Height of wrapping and girth of tree stated		
	4 Temporary fencing			1 Duration and ultimate ownership, details stated
11 Plant containers	1 Method of fixing	1 Dimensioned description	nr	
12 Maintenance	1 Details stated		Item	

M — Measurement rules

M1 Temporary fencing is only measured here where specifically required and then in accordance with Section Q40

D — Definition rules

D1 Types of surface applications include herbicides, selective weedkillers, peat, manure, compost, mulch, fertilizer, soil ameliorants, sand and the like

D2 BS size designations include standard, advanced nursery stock or semi-mature trees

D3 Young nursery stock includes seedlings, transplants and whips

D4 Removing surplus excavated material means removing from site unless otherwise described

C — Coverage rules

C1 Cultivating is deemed to include the removal of stones

C2 Surface applications are deemed to include working in if required

C3 Items include for excavating or forming pits, holes or trenches, refilling, watering in, removing surplus excavated material and labelling

C4 Refilling is deemed to include all necessary multiple handling

C5 Planting in cultivated or grassed areas prepared by others is deemed to include all necessary reinstatement

S — Supplementary information

S1 Timing of operations

S2 Method of cultivating and degree of tilth

S3 Kind, quality and composition of materials

S4 Size and type of pits, holes and trenches, excavated or formed

S5 Type of supports and ties

S6 Special materials for refilling

S7 Labelling

S8 Type of mulch, time and method of application

S9 Type of tree guard and method of fixing

S10 Type of spray and rate of application

S11 Type of wrapping and chemical application

Q40 Fencing

INFORMATION PROVIDED

P1 The following information is shown either on location drawings under A Preliminaries/General conditions or on further drawings which accompany the bills of quantities:
(a) the scope and location of the work
(b) location of fencing specially designed to suit sloping ground

CLASSIFICATION TABLE

			MEASUREMENT RULES	DEFINITION RULES	COVERAGE RULES	SUPPLEMENTARY INFORMATION
						S1 Kind and quality of materials S2 Construction S3 Surface treatments applied as part of production process or applied before delivery to site S4 Size and nature of backfilling
					C1 Work is deemed to include: (a) excavating holes for supports, special supports and independent gate posts (b) backfilling and disposal of surplus materials (c) earthwork support (d) supports	
1 Fencing	1 Height of fencing; spacing, height and depth of supports stated	m 1 Fencing set out to a curve but straight between posts 2 Curved fencing radius > 100 m 3 Curved fencing radius ≤ 100 m, radii stated 4 Fencing to ground sloping > 15° from the horizontal 5 Lengths ≤ 3 m	M1 Fencing is measured over supports and special supports	D1 Supports are posts, struts or the like occurring at regular intervals D2 Special supports are posts, struts or the like other than those occurring at regular intervals D3 The height of fencing is measured from the surface of the ground (or other stated base) to the top of the infilling or where there is no infilling, to the top wire or rail D4 Curved fencing is fencing curved between supports D5 Integral gate posts are those integral with the fencing		
2 Special supports extra over fencing in which they occur	1 End posts 2 Angle posts 3 Integral gate posts 4 Straining posts 5 Others, details stated	nr 1 Method of fixing to background and background stated 2 Details of struts or backstays stated		D6 The height of supports and special supports is the height above the surface of the ground or other stated base D7 The depth of supports and special supports is the depth below the surface of the ground or other stated base	C2 Gate posts are deemed to include slamming stops and hanging fillets	
3 Independent gate posts	1 Type stated	1 Size, height and depth stated				

irrespective of type

				measurements are revised accordingly	
	2 Breaking out existing materials	1 Rock 2 Concrete 3 Reinforced concrete 4 Brickwork, blockwork or stonework 5 Coated macadam or asphalt	m²	D8 Rock is any material which is of such size or position that it can only be removed by wedges, special plant or explosives	
	3 Breaking out existing hard pavings, thickness stated				C4 Making good existing hard pavings is deemed to be included
5 Gates	1 Type stated	1 Height and width stated	nr		C5 Gates are deemed to include gate stops, gate catches and independent gate stays and their associated works
6 Ironmongery				M3 Ironmongery is measured in accordance with Section P21	

R Disposal systems

R10 Rainwater pipework/gutters
R11 Foul drainage above ground

INFORMATION PROVIDED			MEASUREMENT RULES	DEFINITION RULES	COVERAGE RULES	SUPPLEMENTARY INFORMATION
P1 The following information is shown either on location drawings under A Preliminaries/General conditions or on further drawings which accompany the bills of quantities: (a) the scope and location of the work				D1 Finishes and surface treatments exclude insulation and decorative finishes which are measured under Sections Y50 and M60	C1 Providing everything necessary for jointing is deemed to be included C2 Patterns, moulds, templates and the like are deemed to be included	S1 Specified codes of practice and regulations S2 Kind and quality of materials S3 Gauge, thickness or substance of materials S4 Tests with which materials must comply S5 Finishes or surface treatments applied on site S6 Finishes or surface treatments applied off site stating whether applied before or after fabrication or assembly
CLASSIFICATION TABLE						
1 Pipes	1 Straight 2 Curved, radii stated 3 Flexible 4 Extendable	1 Type, nominal size, method of jointing, type, spacing and method of fixing supports, all stated	m	M1 Pipes are measured over all fittings and branches M2 Flexible pipes and extendable pipes are measured fully extended	C3 Pipes are deemed to include joints in their running length C4 Pipes are deemed to include joints necessary solely for erection purposes C5 Pipes are deemed to include all labour excluding made bends	
		1 Background and method of fixing stated 2 In ducts 3 In chases 4 In floor screeds 5 In in situ concrete 6 Bracketed off walls 7 Suspended from soffites				
2 Items extra over the pipe in which they occur	1 Made bends		nr			
	2 Special joints and connections	1 Type, and method of jointing stated				
		1 Nominal size stated where different from pipe in which joint or connection occurs		D2 Special joints and connections are joints which differ from those generally occurring in the running length or are connections to pipes of a different profile or material, connections to		

				in which fitting occurs	which they occur
	3 Three ends				
	4 Others, details stated				
	5 Type stated				
3 Screwed sockets 4 Tappings 5 Bosses	4 Fittings, pipe > 65 mm diameter	1 Type, size and method of jointing stated	nr		C7 Screwed sockets, tappings and bosses are deemed to include perforating the pipe
					C8 Cutting and jointing pipes to ancillaries is deemed to be included
6 Pipework ancillaries	1 Gullies 2 Outlets 3 Rainwater heads 4 Gratings to outlets and rainwater heads 5 Flashing plates 6 Weathering aprons 7 Tundishes 8 Traps 9 Pots	1 Type, nominal size, type of pipe and method of fixing any supports stated	nr	1 Background and method of fixing stated 2 In ducts	M4 Gratings may alternatively be given in the description of the enumerated item to which they relate
7 Pipe supports which differ from those given with pipelines		1 Nominal size of pipe, type and size of support, method of fixing pipe and support stated	nr	1 Lined with insulation, details stated 2 Background and method of fixing stated	M5 Fabricated supports and supports carrying more than one service are measured under Section P30/31
8 Pipe sleeves through walls, floors and ceilings	1 Length ≤ 300 mm 2 and thereafter in 300 mm stages	1 Type and nominal size of pipe stated	nr	1 Method of fixing and type of packing stated 2 Handed to others for fixing	
9 Wall, floor and ceiling plates		1 Type, size and method of fixing stated	nr		

R10/R11 continued

CLASSIFICATION TABLE				MEASUREMENT RULES	DEFINITION RULES	COVERAGE RULES	SUPPLEMENTARY INFORMATION
10 Gutters	1 Straight 2 Curved, radii stated		m	1 Type, nominal size, method of jointing, type, spacing and method of fixing supports stated	1 Background and method of fixing stated	M6 Gutters are measured over all fittings and branches	C9 Gutters are deemed to include joints in the running length	
11 Items extra over the gutter in which they occur	1 Special joints and connections		nr	1 Type and method of jointing stated	1 Nominal size stated where different from gutter in which joint or connection occurs		D3 Special joints and connections are joints which differ from those generally occurring in the running length or are connections to existing gutter or gutters of a different profile or material	
	2 Fittings			1 Type stated	1 Method of jointing stated where different from gutter in which fitting occurs	M7 Fittings which are reducing are measured extra over the largest gutters in which they occur	C10 Cutting and jointing gutters to fittings is deemed to be included	
12 Marking position of holes, mortices and chases in the structure	1 Installation stated		item		1 Formed during construction, details stated			
13 Identification	1 Plates 2 Discs 3 Labels 4 Tapes or bands 5 Arrows, symbols, letters and numbers 6 Charts		nr	1 Type, size and method of fixing stated	1 Details of engraving stated 2 Mounting of charts, details stated			
14 Testing and commissioning	1 Installation stated		item	1 Preparatory operations, details stated 2 Stage tests (nr) listed and purpose stated 3 Insurance Company tests, details stated 4 Instruction of personnel in operation of completed installation	1 Attendance required 2 Instruments to be provided		C11 Provision of water, and other supplies are deemed to be included C12 Provision of test certificates is deemed to be included	
15 Temporary operation of installations to Employer's requirements	1 Installation and purpose of operation stated		item	1 Duration of operation period stated	1 Attendance required 2 Conditions imposed by Employer before operation allowed	M8 Provision of water, fuel, gas, electricity and other supplies is covered by Provisional Sums in Section A54		

manufacturers and
installation drawings and
record or 'as fitted' drawings

2 Names of recipients
stated

17 Operating and
maintenance manuals

R12 Drainage below ground
R13 Land drainage

INFORMATION PROVIDED							SUPPLEMENTARY INFORMATION

P1 Information regarding the nature of excavation work is described in accordance with Section D20 Information Provided
P2 The following information is shown either on location drawings under A Preliminaries/General conditions or on further drawings which accompany the bills of quantities:
  (a) the layout of the drainage

CLASSIFICATION TABLE

			MEASUREMENT RULES	DEFINITION RULES	COVERAGE RULES	SUPPLEMENTARY INFORMATION
1 Excavating trenches	1 Pipes ≤ 200 mm nominal size 2 Pipes > 200 mm nominal size, nominal size stated	m	1 Average depth of trench ≤ 250 mm 2 and thereafter in 250 mm stages 1 Commencing level stated where >0.25 mm below existing ground level 2 Curved 3 Below ground water level 4 Next to roadways 5 Next to existing buildings 6 Unstable ground 7 Specified multiple handling, details stated 8 Disposal at specified locations, details stated 9 Backfilling with special materials, details stated 10 Surface treatments, details stated 11 Active material 12 Toxic/hazardous material, type stated	M1 Special materials for backfilling are stated in accordance with D20:9.∗.∗.∗ M2 Surface treatments are stated in accordance with D20:13.∗.∗.∗ M3 Excavating trenches below ground water level is measured where the ground water level is above the bottom of the trench	D1 A run of pipe trench is an uninterrupted line of excavating such as between manholes or between an accessory and a manhole or between accessories D2 Trenches next to roadways, next to existing buildings, and in unstable ground are defined in accordance with D20:7.∗.∗.3–5 D3 Backfilling with special materials occurs where selected or treated excavated materials, or imported materials are used D4 Active, toxic/hazardous material as defined Section D20 Rules D2 and D3	C1 Excavating trenches is deemed to include: (a) earthwork support (b) consolidation of trench bottoms (c) trimming excavations (d) filling with and compaction of general filling materials (e) disposal of surplus excavated materials	S2 Specified protection where specified
2 Items extra over excavating trenches, irrespective of depth	1 Breaking out existing materials 2 Concrete	m³	1 Rock 2 Concrete	M4 The measurement of extra over items is based on the width of the beds in the trenches. Where there are no beds the width to be taken is the nominal size of the service plus 300 mm. In both cases measurement is subject to a minimum width of 500 mm	D5 Rock is any material which is of such size or position that it can only be removed by wedges, special plant or explosives	
	2 Breaking out existing hard pavings, thickness stated	m²	3 Reinforced concrete 4 Brickwork, blockwork or stonework 5 Coated macadam or asphalt 1 Reinstating to match existing			
	3 Lifting turf for preservation		1 Method of preserving, details stated			

Classification			Unit	Supplementary information	Measurement rules	Definition rules	Coverage rules
7 Around existing live services crossing trench			nr				
3 Disposal	1 Surface water		item		M6 An item for disposal of ground water is only measured where a corresponding item is measured in accordance with 1.*.*.3 and is adjusted accordingly if the post contract water level is different		
	2 Ground water						
4 Beds	1 Width and thickness of bed stated	1 Nominal size of pipe stated	m			1 Designed joints, details stated	C2 Beds, haunchings, surrounds and casings are deemed to include formwork
5 Beds and haunchings							
6 Beds and surrounds	1 Width, thickness of bed and thickness of surround stated						
7 Vertical casings	1 Size stated						
8 Pipes	1 In trenches	1 Nominal size stated	m	1 Iron pipes in runs ≤ 3 m long (nr)	M7 Pipes are measured over all fittings and branches		C3 Pipes are deemed to include pipe supports
	2 In ducts			2 Not laid in bottom of trench, average depth stated in accordance with 1.*.*.*			
				3 Vertical			
				4 Height > 3.50 m above floor level			S4 Method of jointing pipes
9 Items extra over the pipe in which they occur	1 Pipe fittings	1 Description stated	nr				C4 Pipe fittings are deemed to include cutting and jointing pipes to fittings and providing everything necessary for jointing
10 Pipe accessories	1 Type stated	1 Dimensioned description	nr			D7 Accessories include gullies, traps, inspection shoes, fresh air inlets, non-return flaps and the like	C5 Accessories are deemed to include jointing pipes thereto and bedding in concrete
						D8 Dimensions stated for accessories include the nominal size of each inlet and outlet	S5 Method of jointing fittings and accessories to pipes

R12/R13 continued

CLASSIFICATION TABLE				MEASUREMENT RULES	DEFINITION RULES	COVERAGE RULES	SUPPLEMENTARY INFORMATION
11 Manholes 12 Inspection chambers 13 Soakaways 14 Cesspits 15 Septic tanks	1 Excavation 2 Concrete 3 Formwork 4 Reinforcement 5 Brickwork 6 Rendered coatings			M8 Excavation, concrete, formwork, brickwork, rendered coatings and other work are measured in accordance with the rules for the appropriate Work Sections			
	7 Building in ends of pipes 8 Channels 9 Benching 10 Step irons 11 Covers 12 Intercepting traps 13 Others	1 Dimensioned description	nr	M9 Items 11–15.7–13.1.0 are only measured separately in non preformed systems		C6 Building in ends of pipes is deemed to include cutting pipes	
	14 Preformed systems	1 Details stated	nr	1 Building in ends of pipes, details stated 2 Channels, details stated 3 Benching, details stated 4 Step irons, details stated 5 Covers, details stated 6 Intercepting traps, details stated			
16 Connecting to Local Authority's sewer	1 Details stated		nr	M10 Connecting to Local Authority's sewer is only measured here where it is executed by the Contractor. Work by Statutory Authorities is measured in Section A53			
17 Testing and commissioning	1 Installation stated	1 Preparatory operations, details stated 2 Stage tests (nr) listed and purpose stated 3 Insurance Company tests, details stated 4 Instruction of personnel in operation of completed installations	item			C7 Provision of water and other supplies is deemed to be included C8 Provision of test certificates is deemed to be included	
		1 Attendance required 2 Instruments to be provided					

installation drawings and record or 'as fitted' drawings

2 Names of recipients stated

19 Operating and maintenance manuals

X Transport systems

INFORMATION PROVIDED	MEASUREMENT RULES	DEFINITION RULES	COVERAGE RULES	SUPPLEMENTARY INFORMATION
P1 The following information is shown either on location drawings under A Preliminaries/General conditions or on further drawings which accompany the bills of quantities: (a) the scope and location of the work, including extent of work in motor, machinery or plant rooms	M1 It is permissible in respect of any individual item to use any other appropriate Rule in this document provided that it is stated which Rules have been applied to the item			S1 Such information as is appropriate to the procurement, design, execution, supply and/or manufacture of the item and its incorporation in the works

CLASSIFICATION TABLE

				MEASUREMENT RULES	DEFINITION RULES	COVERAGE RULES	SUPPLEMENTARY INFORMATION
1 Lifts 2 Escalators 3 Moving pavements 4 Powered stairlifts 5 Fire escape chutes/slings 6 Hoists 7 Cranes 8 Travelling cradles, gantries, ladders 9 Goods distribution/ Mechanised warehousing 10 Mechanical document conveying 11 Pneumatic document conveying 12 Automatic document filing and retrieval	1 Component drawing reference 2 Type, size, pattern, capacity, loading, length, floors served as appropriate, all stated	1 Cross reference to specification	nr	M2 Work is classified in accordance with the following Work Sections and given under an appropriate Work Section heading: X10 Lifts X11 Escalators X12 Moving pavements X13 Powered stair lifts X14 Fire escape chutes/ slings X20 Hoists X21 Cranes X22 Travelling cradles, gantries, ladders X23 Goods distribution/ Mechanised warehousing X30 Mechanical document conveying X31 Pneumatic document conveying X32 Automatic document filing and retrieval			
13 Marking position of holes, mortices and chases in the structure	1 Installation stated		item	1 Formed during construction, details stated			
14 Identification where not provided with equipment	1 Plates 2 Discs 3 Labels 4 Tapes or bands 5 Arrows, symbols, letters and numbers 6 Charts	1 Type, size and method of fixing stated	nr	1 Details of engraving stated 2 Mounting of charts, details stated			

					C2 Provision of test certificates is deemed to be included
			purpose stated		
			3 Insurance Company tests, details stated		
			4 Instruction of personnel in operation of completed installation		
16 Temporary operation of installations to Employer's requirements	1 Installation and purpose of operation stated	1 Duration of operation period stated	item	1 Attendance required	M3 Provision of electricity and other supplies is covered by Provisional Sums in Section A54
				2 Conditions imposed by Employer before operation allowed	
				3 Special insurance requirements of Employer stated	
17 Preparing drawings	1 Information required and number of copies stated	1 Negatives, prints and microfilms, details stated	item	1 Binding into sets, details stated	D1 Drawings include builder's work, manufacturer's and installation drawings and record or 'as fitted' drawings
				2 Names of recipients stated	
18 Operating and maintenance manuals					

Y Mechanical and electrical services measurement

Y10 Pipelines
Y11 Pipeline ancillaries

INFORMATION PROVIDED			MEASUREMENT RULES	DEFINITION RULES	COVERAGE RULES	SUPPLEMENTARY INFORMATION
P1 The following information is shown either on location drawings under A Preliminaries/General conditions or on further drawings (a) scope and location of the work including extent of work in plant rooms			M1 Work related to these Sections is classified in accordance with Sections R14 and R20–U70 as Appendix B and given under an appropriate Work Section heading M2 Work in plant rooms is identified separately	D1 Finishes and surface treatments exclude insulation and decorative finishes which are measured under Sections Y50 and M60	C1 Providing everything necessary for jointing is deemed to be included C2 Patterns, moulds, templates and the like are deemed to be included	S1 Specified codes of practice and regulations S2 Kind and quality of materials S3 Gauge, thickness or substance of materials S4 Tests with which materials must comply S5 Finishes or surface treatments applied on site S6 Finishes or surface treatments applied off site stating whether applied before or after fabrication or assembly

CLASSIFICATION TABLE

					MEASUREMENT RULES		COVERAGE RULES	
1 Pipes	1 Straight 2 Curved, radii stated 3 Flexible 4 Extendable	m	1 Background stated 2 In ducts 3 In trenches 4 In chases 5 In floor screeds 6 In in situ concrete		M3 Pipes are measured over all fittings and branches M4 Flexible and extendable pipes are measured fully extended		C3 Pipes are deemed to include joints in their running length C4 Pipes are deemed to include joints necessary solely for erection purposes	
	5 Flow and return header pipes	nr	2 Type, length and nominal size of main pipe, number, type, length and diameter of each branch pipe, method of construction and method of jointing ends, type, number and method of fixing supports stated					

					Measurement rules	Coverage rules
connections			...which joint or connection occurs			...length or are connections to pipes of a different profile or material, connections to existing pipes or to equipment, appliances or ends of flue pipes
3 Fittings, pipe ≤ 65 mm diameter,			2 One end 3 Two ends 4 Three ends 5 Others, details stated			C5 Cutting and jointing pipes to fittings, loops and compensators is deemed to be included
4 Fittings, pipe > 65 mm diameter			6 Type stated		M5 Fittings which are reducing are measured extra over the largest pipe in which they occur	
3 Expansion loops	Type, nominal size, method of jointing, type, number and method of fixing supports stated	nr	1 Limiting dimensions and expansion accommodated stated	1 Background stated 2 In ducts 3 In trenches		
4 Expansion compensators		nr	1 Expansion accommodated stated			
5 Screwed sockets 6 Tappings 7 Bosses	Type, size and method of jointing stated	nr	1 Nominal size and kind of pipe stated			C6 Screwed sockets, tappings and bosses are deemed to include perforating the pipe
8 Pipework ancillaries	Type, nominal size, method of jointing, type, number and method of fixing supports all stated	nr	1 Type of pipe stated	1 Integral controls or indicators stated 2 Remote controls or indicators and connections between stated 3 Background stated 4 In ducts 5 In trenches		C7 Cutting and jointing pipes to ancillaries is deemed to be included

Y10, Y11 continued

CLASSIFICATION TABLE				MEASUREMENT RULES	DEFINITION RULES	COVERAGE RULES	SUPPLEMENTARY INFORMATION
9 Pipe supports which differ from those given with pipelines		1 Nominal size of pipe, type and size of support, method of fixing pipe and support stated	nr	1 Lined with insulation, details stated 2 Spring compensated, loading and movement accommodated stated 3 Background stated	M6 Fabricated supports and supports carrying more than one service are measured in Section P31		
10 Pipe anchors and guides		1 Nominal size of pipe, type, size and composition, method of fixing pipe and anchors or guide stated	nr				
11 Pipe sleeves through walls, floors and ceilings	1 Length ≤ 300 mm 2 and thereafter in 300 mm stages	1 Type and nominal size of pipe stated	nr	1 Method of fixing and type of packing stated 2 Handed to others for fixing			
12 Wall, floor and ceiling plates		1 Type, size and method of fixing stated	nr				

Y52 Vibration isolation mountings
Y53 Control components - mechanical

INFORMATION PROVIDED	MEASUREMENT RULES	DEFINITION RULES	COVERAGE RULES	SUPPLEMENTARY INFORMATION
P1 The following information is shown either on location drawings under A Preliminaries/General conditions or on further drawings which accompany the bills of quantities: (a) scope and location of the work including extent of work in plant rooms	M1 Work related to these Sections is classified in accordance with Sections R14 – U70 as Appendix B and given under an appropriate Work Section heading M2 Work in plant rooms is identified separately	D1 Finishes and surface treatments exclude insulation and decorative finishes which are measured under Sections Y50 and M60	C1 Providing everything necessary for jointing is deemed to be included C2 Patterns, moulds, templates and the like are deemed to be included	S1 Specified codes of practice and regulations S2 Kind and quality of materials S3 Gauge, thickness or substance of materials S4 Tests with which materials and equipment must comply S5 Finishes or surface treatments applied on site S6 Finishes or surface treatments applied off site stating whether applied before or after fabrication or assembly S7 Limiting dimensions on the size and weight of equipment

CLASSIFICATION TABLE

1 Equipment	1 Type, size and pattern, rated duty, capacity, loading as appropriate and method of fixing all stated	1 Cross-reference to Specification	nr
			1 Ancillaries provided with equipment, details stated
			2 Integral controls or indicators, details stated
			3 Remote controls or indicators, and connections between, details stated
			4 Supports, anti-vibration mountings, insulation provided with equipment, details and method of fixing stated
			5 Initial charges, details stated
			6 Background stated

C3 Plates, discs and labels for identification provided with the equipment are deemed to be included

Y20-Y25/Y40-Y46/Y52/Y53 continued

CLASSIFICATION TABLE		Unit		MEASUREMENT RULES	DEFINITION RULES	COVERAGE RULES	SUPPLEMENTARY INFORMATION
2 Ancillaries for equipment not provided with the equipment	1 Type, size and method of jointing stated	nr	1 Integral controls or indicators, details stated 2 Remote controls or indicators, and connections between, details stated			C4 Jointing ancillaries to equipment is deemed to be included	
3 Sill heaters 4 Skirting heaters	1 Elements (nr)	m	1 Output, type, size and method of jointing stated			C5 Edge sealing strips are deemed to be included	
	2 Casings	m	2 Type, size and method of jointing stated				
5 Items extra over the sill or skirting heater casings in which they occur	1 Angle sections 2 Matching plates 3 Valve access covers 4 End covers	nr	1 Type, size and method of jointing stated				
6 Supports where not provided with the equipment	1 Type, size and method of fixing stated	nr	1 Background stated				
7 Independent vertical steel chimneys	1 Height, internal diameter and method of jointing stated	nr	1 Base plates (nr) 2 Base plate templates (nr) 3 Linings (nr) 4 Claddings (nr) 5 Anchor bolts (nr) 6 Guy ropes (nr) 7 Ladders (nr) 8 Guard rails (nr) 9 Painters hooks (nr) 10 Cleaning doors (nr) 11 Cowls 12 Terminals	M3 Flue pipes are measured as pipelines in Section Y10			
8 Anti vibration mountings where not provided with the equipment	1 Type, size and method of fixing stated	nr	1 Background stated				
9 Anti vibration or sound insulation material	1 Plant bases	m²	1 Nature and thickness stated	1 Handed to others for fixing			

INFORMATION PROVIDED	MEASUREMENT RULES	DEFINITION RULES	COVERAGE RULES	SUPPLEMENTARY INFORMATION
P1 The following information is shown either on location drawings under A Preliminaries/General conditions or on further drawings which accompany the bills of quantities: (a) scope and location of the work, including extent of work in plant rooms	M1 Work related to this Section is classified in accordance with Sections U10 – U70 as Appendix B and given under an appropriate Work Section heading M2 Work in plant rooms is identified separately	D1 Finishes and surface treatments exclude insulation and decorative finishes which are measured under Sections Y50 and M60	C1 Providing everything necessary for jointing is deemed to be included C2 Patterns, moulds templates and the like are deemed to be included	S1 Specified codes of practice and regulations S2 Kind and quality of materials S3 Gauge, thickness or substance of materials S4 Tests with which materials must comply S5 Finishes or surface treatments applied on site S6 Finishes or surface treatments applied off site stating whether applied before or after fabrication or assembly

CLASSIFICATION TABLE

Item	Sub-classification	Information required	Unit	Supplementary	MEASUREMENT RULES	DEFINITION RULES	COVERAGE RULES
1 Ducting	1 Straight 2 Curved, radii stated 3 Rectangular curved on wider side, radii stated 4 Rectangular curved on narrower side, radii stated 5 Flexible	1 Type, shape, size, method of jointing type, spacing and method of fixing supports stated	m	1 Background stated	M3 Ducting is measured over all fittings and branches		C3 Ducting is deemed to include: (a) joints in the running length (b) stiffeners
2 Items extra over the ducting in which they occur	1 Lining ducting internally	1 Type and thickness of lining material and internal size of ducting stated	m		M4 Lining may alternatively be given in the description of the ducting		
	2 Special joints and connections	1 Type, size, ducting size and method of jointing stated	nr	1 Size stated where different from duct in which joint or connection occurs	M5 Where there is a preponderance of fittings (e.g. in plant rooms) they may be enumerated separately as individual full cost items	D2 Special joints and connections are joints which differ from those generally occurring in the running length or are connections to ducting of a different profile or material or to equipment and appliances	
	3 Fittings 4 Access openings and covers or doors 5 Nozzle outlets 6 Test holes and covers	1 Method of jointing stated where different from duct in which fitting occurs	nr	1 Type stated			C4 Access openings, nozzle outlets and test holes are deemed to include the stiffening of openings C5 Cutting and jointing ducts to fittings is deemed to be included
3 Turns and splitters where not provided with fittings	1 Type stated	1 Internal size of ducting stated	nr				

Y30 continued

CLASSIFICATION TABLE				MEASUREMENT RULES	DEFINITION RULES	COVERAGE RULES	SUPPLEMENTARY INFORMATION
4 Ancillaries	1 Type, size, method of jointing, type, number and method of fixing supports all stated	nr	1 Type of ducting stated 2 Remote controls and indicators and connections between, details stated 3 Background stated			C6 Cutting and jointing ducts to ancillaries is deemed to be included	
			1 Integral controls and indicators, details stated				
5 Breaking into existing ducts	1 Type, size and location of duct stated	item	1 Purpose of breaking in stated				
			1 Obtaining approval for isolation where necessary 2 Isolating existing duct 3 Preparing ends of existing for new work 4 Limitations to shut down period				
6 Ducting supports which differ from those given with ductline	1 Shape, size of duct, type and size of support, method of fixing duct and support stated	nr	1 Lined with insulation, details stated 2 Spring compensated, loading and movement accommodated stated 3 Background stated	M6 Fabricated supports and supports carrying more than one service are measured in Section P31			
7 Ducting sleeves through walls, floors and ceilings	1 ≤ 300 mm length 2 and thereafter in 300 mm stages	nr	1 Type and size of ducting stated				
			1 Method of fixing and type of packing stated 2 Handed to others for fixing				

INFORMATION PROVIDED

P1 The following information is shown either on location drawings under A Preliminaries/General conditions or on further drawings which accompany the bills of quantities:
(a) scope and location of the work including extent of work in plant rooms

CLASSIFICATION TABLE

First division	Second division	Unit	Third division	
1 Insulation, type stated	1 Pipelines	m	1 Nominal size of pipeline stated	1 Flanged pipelines 2 Traced oil pipelines 3 Smoke pipelines 4 Flue pipelines
	2 Insulation boxes for pipelines	nr	1 Type of infill stated	
	3 Air ductlines	m	1 Nominal size of ductline stated	
	4 Equipment	m²	1 Insulation contained in casings of specific dimensions	
		nr	2 Overall size stated	
2 Items extra over insulation	1 Pipelines	nr	1 Working around ancillaries	
	2 Air ductlines		2 Boxes for valves, details stated	
	3 Equipment		3 Detachable mattresses	
			4 Working around ancillaries	
	4 Pipeline and air ductline fittings where insulation has metal clad facing		5 Details stated	
3 Loose or cellular concrete insulation	1 In trenches, ducts, tank casings and the like	m³	1 Special protection or finish at openings through walls, valve chambers and the like included, details stated	

MEASUREMENT RULES

M1 Work related to this Section is classified in accordance with Sections R14 – U70 as Appendix B and given under an appropriate Work Section heading

M2 Work in plant rooms is identified separately

M3 Equipment insulation measured superficially is measured on the surface of the insulants

M4 Alternatively items relating to equipment insulation may be given in the description of the enumerated items concerned

COVERAGE RULES

C1 Insulation is deemed to include:
(a) smoothing the materials and working around supports
(b) working around pipe flanges
(c) working around fittings excluding metal clad facing insulants

SUPPLEMENTARY INFORMATION

S1 Specified under codes of practice and regulations
S2 Kind and quality of materials
S3 Thickness of materials
S4 Coatings and facings
S5 Method of fixing

Y51 Testing and commissioning mechanical services
Y54 Identification - mechanical
Y59 Sundry common mechanical items

INFORMATION PROVIDED			MEASUREMENT RULES	DEFINITION RULES	COVERAGE RULES	SUPPLEMENTARY INFORMATION
P1 Information is shown on location drawings under A Preliminaries/General conditions			M1 Work related to this Section is classified in accordance with Sections R14 – U70 as Appendix B and given under an appropriate Work Section heading			
CLASSIFICATION TABLE						
1 Marking position of holes, mortices and chases in the structure	item	1 Formed during construction, details stated				
2 Loose ancillaries	nr	1 Name of recipient stated				
1 Keys						
2 Tools						
3 Spares						
4 Parts/chemicals						
3 Identification where not provided with equipment or ancillaries	nr	1 Type, size and method of fixing stated				
1 Plates		1 Details of engraving stated				
2 Discs		2 Mounting of charts, details stated				
3 Labels						
4 Tapes or bands						
5 Arrows, symbols, letters and numbers						
6 Charts						
4 Testing and commissioning	item	1 Attendance required				
1 Installation stated		2 Instruments to be provided				
1 Preparatory operations, details stated						
2 Stage tests (nr) listed and purpose stated						
3 Insurance Company tests, details stated						
4 Instruction of personnel in operation of completed installation						
5 Temporary operation of installations to Employer's requirements	item	1 Attendance required	M2 Provision of water, fuel, gas, electricity and other supplies is covered by Provisional Sums in Section		C1 Provision of water, fuel, gas, electricity and other supplies is deemed to be included	
1 Installation and purpose of operation stated		2 Conditions imposed by Employer before operation allowed			C2 Provision of test certificates is deemed to be included	
1 Duration of operation period stated						

	item		installation drawings and record or 'as fitted' drawings
7 Operating and maintenance manuals		2 Names of recipients stated	

Y60 Conduit and cable trunking
Y63 Support components - cables

INFORMATION PROVIDED	MEASUREMENT RULES	DEFINITION RULES	COVERAGE RULES	SUPPLEMENTARY INFORMATION
P1 The following information is shown either on location drawings under A Preliminaries/General conditions or on further drawings which accompany the bills of quantities: (a) scope and location of the work	M1 **Work related to these Sections is classified in accordance with Sections V10 – W60 as Appendix B and given under an appropriate Work Section heading**	D1 Finishes and surface treatments exclude decorative finishes which are measured under Section M60	C1 Providing everything necessary for jointing is deemed to be included C2 Patterns, moulds, templates and the like are deemed to be included	S1 Specified codes of practice and regulations S2 Kind and quality of materials S3 Gauge thickness or substance of materials S4 Tests with which materials must comply S5 Finishes or surface treatments applied on site S6 Finishes or surface treatments applied off site stating whether applied before or after fabrication or assembly

CLASSIFICATION TABLE

					MEASUREMENT RULES	COVERAGE RULES
1 Conduit	1 Straight 2 Curved, radii stated	m	1 Background stated 2 To surfaces 3 In chases 4 In floor screeds 5 In situ concrete	1 Type and external size and method of fixing stated	M2 Conduit is measured over all conduit fittings and branches M3 Independent earth conductors are measured separately under Section Y61 or Y80	C3 Conduit is deemed to include: (a) bending, cutting, screwing, jointing and all conduit fittings excluding 2.*.1.* (b) clips, saddles and crampets (c) forming holes for conduit entry (d) draw wires, draw cables, and the like (e) components for earth continuity
	3 Flexible connections 4 Extendable connections	nr	1 Earthing tails	1 Type, size, overall length and type of adaptors stated		C4 Cutting and jointing conduit to boxes is deemed to be included
2 Items extra over the conduit in which they occur	1 Special boxes 2 Adaptable boxes 3 Floor trap boxes 4 Purpose made boxes 5 Rectangular junction boxes 6 Expansion joints	nr	1 Background stated	1 Type, size, cover and method of fixing stated		

4 Connections of conduit to equipment and control gear					
5 Cable trunking	1 Straight 2 Curved, radii stated	m	1 Type, size, method of jointing and type, spacing and method of fixing supports all stated	1 Background stated 2 Pin racks 3 Compartments (nr), size stated	M4 Cable trunking is measured over all fittings and branches M5 Independent earth conductors are measured separately under Sections Y61 and Y80	C5 Trunking is deemed to include components for earth continuity
6 Item extra over the cable trunking in which they occur	1 Fittings	nr	1 Type stated	1 Bushing material, type and size stated		C6 Cutting and jointing trunking to fittings is deemed to be included
7 Connections of cable trunking to equipment and control gear	1 Forming holes	nr	1 Size of opening stated			
	2 With flanges 3 With flanges and forming holes	nr	2 Size of opening and type and size of flanges stated			
8 Cable tray, ladders and racks	1 Straight 2 Curved, radii stated	m	1 Type, width, method of jointing and type spacing and method of fixing supports, all stated	1 Background stated	M6 Cable tray, ladders and racks are measured over all fittings and branches M7 Independent earth conductors are measusred separately under Sections Y61 or Y80	C7 Cable tray is deemed to include components for earth continuity
9 Cable tray stools	1 Type and size stated	nr				
10 Items extra over the cable tray, ladders and racks in which they occur	1 Fittings	nr				C8 Cutting and jointing tray to fittings is deemed to be included
11 Supports for cable trunking	1 Supports which differ from those given with the trunking or cable tray, ladders and racks	nr	1 Size of trunking, tray ladder or rack, type and size of support, method of fixing trunking, tray, ladder or rack and support all stated	1 Background stated		
12 Supports for cable tray, ladders and racks						

Y61 HV/LV cables and wiring
Y62 Busbar trunking
Y80 Earthing and bonding components

INFORMATION PROVIDED

P1 The following information is shown either on location drawings under A Preliminaries/General conditions or on further drawings which accompany the bills of quantities:
  (a) scope and location of the work

P2 The following information regarding final circuits is given:
  (a) a distribution sheet setting out the number and location of all fittings and accessories
  (b) a location drawing showing the layout of the points

CLASSIFICATION TABLE			MEASUREMENT RULES	DEFINITION RULES	COVERAGE RULES	SUPPLEMENTARY INFORMATION
			M1 Work related to these Sections is classified in accordance with Sections V10 – W60 as Appendix B and given under an appropriate Work Section heading	D1 Finishes and surface treatments exclude decorative finishes which are measured in Section M60	C1 Providing everything necessary for jointing is deemed to be included C2 Patterns, moulds, templates and the like are deemed to be included	S1 Specified codes of practice and regulations S2 Kind and quality of materials S3 Gauge, thickness or substance of materials S4 Tests with which materials must comply S5 Finishes or surface treatments applied on site S6 Finishes or surface treatment applied off site stating whether applied before or after fabrication or assembly S7 Details of colour coding or other markings of cables for phase identification
1 Cables	1 Type, size, number of cores, armouring and sheathing stated	m	1 Drawn into conduits or ducts or laid or drawn into trunking 2 Laid or drawn into trunking and laced into circuit groups 3 Fixed to surfaces 4 Wrapped around pipework 5 Laid in trenches 6 Fixed to insulators in overhead lines 7 Suspended from catenary cables	1 Type, spacing and method of fixing supports stated 2 Background stated	M2 Cables in conduits or trunking and cables fixed to trays are measured as the net length of the conduit, trunking or tray. Other cables are measured as fixed without allowance for sag M3 The following allowances shall be made to those cables measured net: (a) 0.30 m on each cable entering fittings, luminaries or accessories (b) 0.60 m on each cable entering equipment or control gear	D2 Cables are defined as being laced into circuit groups where this is specified	C3 Cables are deemed to include: (a) wall, floor and ceiling plates (b) cable sleeves (c) connecting tails	
2 Flexible cable connections	1 Type, size, number of cores, armouring, sheathing, capacity stated, length ≤ 1.00 m	nr	1 Details of connections at each end stated				

4 Line taps				1 Shrouds, type stated		
5 Cable termination glands	1 Type and size of cable, and type of gland stated	1 Box, type, size and method of fixing stated	nr	1 Cable connector blocks, type and size stated		
6 Cable supports which differ from those given with cables	1 Size of cable, type and size of support and method of fixing stated	1 Fixed to surfaces 2 Fixed to conductors in overhead lines 3 Suspended from catenary cables	nr	1 Background stated		
7 Busbar trunking	1 Type, size, cover, method of jointing, number and rated capacity of busbars and type, spacing and method of fixing supports all stated	1 Straight 2 Curved, radii stated	m	1 Background stated	M4 Busbar trunking is measured over all fittings and branches	
8 Items extra over the busbar trunking in which they occur	1 Fittings	1 Type stated	nr			C4 Cutting and jointing busbar trunking to fittings, tap off units, feeder units and fire barriers is deemed to be included
9 Tap off units 10 Feeder units 11 Fire barriers	1 Type, size and method of fixing stated	1 Rated capacity stated	nr	1 Background stated		
12 Busbar trunking supports which differ from those given with busbar trunking	1 Size of trunking, type and size of support and method of fixing stated		nr			
13 Tapes	1 Type and size of tape, type and spacing of fixings and method of fixing stated	1 Type and size of tape, type and spacing of fixings and method of fixing stated	m		M5 13 – 18.$*$.0.$*$ are only measured in relation to Section Y80	
14 Connections 15 Junctions	1 Type and size of tape stated		nr			
16 Test clamps	1 Type, size and method of connecting stated					
17 Electrodes	1 Type and size stated			1 Driving into the ground		
18 Air termination points	1 Type, size and method of fixing stated			1 Background stated		C5 Cutting and jointing tapes to connectors, junctions, clamps, electrodes and air termination points is deemed to be included

Y61/Y62/Y80 continued

CLASSIFICATION TABLE				MEASUREMENT RULES	DEFINITION RULES	COVERAGE RULES	SUPPLEMENTARY INFORMATION
19 Cable and conduit in final circuits	1 Cable installation, size and type of cable, and description of final circuit stated 2 Cable and conduit installation, size and type of conduit, and description of final circuit stated	nr	1 Cables and protective conductors for earthing 2 Special boxes 3 Surface 4 Concealed 5 Background and method of fixing stated 1 Sockets, switch sockets and the like 2 Immersion heaters, cooker outlets and the like 3 Lighting outlets 4 One way switches 5 Two way switches 6 Intermediate switches	M6 Final circuits not forming part of a domestic or similar simple installation from distribution boards and the like are kept separate and measured in detail in accordance with Sections Y60 & Y63 and Sections Y61, Y62 & Y80: 1 – 18∗.∗∗ M7 Final circuits are measured on an enumerated points basis where they form part of a domestic or similar simple installation from distribution boards and the like M8 Each lighting outlet is measured as one point irrespective of the number of lamps M9 Cables and protective conductors for earthing are only given in the description where they form an integral part of the final circuit M10 Special boxes given in the description are specifically required boxes which differ from those included in C5		C6 Final circuits measured on an enumerated points basis are deemed to include: (a) conduit accessories including conduit boxes required for the particular type of installation (b) fixing, bending, cutting, screwing and jointing (c) determining routes	S8 Voltage and amperage

Y72 Contactors and starters
Y92 Motor drives - electric

INFORMATION PROVIDED	MEASUREMENT RULES	DEFINITION RULES	COVERAGE RULES	SUPPLEMENTARY INFORMATION
P1 The following information is shown either on location drawings under A Preliminaries/General conditions or on further drawings which accompany the bills of quantities: (a) scope and location of the work	M1 **Work related to these Sections is classified in accordance with Sections V10 – W60 as Appendix B and given under an appropriate Work Section heading**	D1 Finishes and surface treatments exclude decorative finishes which are measured in Section M60	C1 Providing everything necessary for jointing is deemed to be included C2 Patterns, moulds, templates and the like are deemed to be included	S1 Specified codes of practice and regulations S2 Kind and quality of material S3 Gauge, thickness or substance of materials S4 Tests with which materials must comply S5 Finishes or surface treatments applied on site S6 Finishes and surface treatments applied off site stating whether applied before or after fabrication or assembly S7 Limiting dimensions on the size and weight of the equipment
			C3 Plates, discs and labels for identification provided with the equipment are deemed to be included	

CLASSIFICATION TABLE

1 Switchgear 2 Distribution boards 3 Contactors and starters 4 Motor drives	1 Type, size, rated capacity and method of fixing stated	1 Cross reference to Specification	nr	1 Fuses 2 Supports provided with the equipment, details and method of fixing stated 3 Background stated
5 Supports where not provided with switchgear, distribution boards, contactors and starters, or motor drives	1 Type, size and method of fixing stated		nr	1 Background stated

Y73 Luminaires and lamps
Y74 Accessories for electrical services

INFORMATION PROVIDED				MEASUREMENT RULES	DEFINITION RULES	COVERAGE RULES	SUPPLEMENTARY INFORMATION
P1 The following information is shown either on location drawings under A Preliminaries/General conditions or on further drawings which accompany the bills of quantities: (a) scope and location of the work				M1 Work related to these Sections is classified in accordance with Sections V10 – W60 as Appendix B and given under an appropriate Work Section heading	D1 Finishes and surface treatments exclude decorative finishes which are measured under Section M60	C1 Providing everything necessary for jointing is deemed to be included C2 Patterns, moulds, templates and the like are deemed to be included	S1 Specified codes of practice and regulations S2 Kind and quality of materials S3 Gauge, thickness or substance of materials S4 Tests with which materials must comply S5 Finishes or surface treatments applied on site S6 Finishes or surface treatments applied off site stating whether applied before or after fabrication or assembly

CLASSIFICATION TABLE

				MEASUREMENT RULES	DEFINITION RULES	COVERAGE RULES	SUPPLEMENTARY INFORMATION
1 Particular specification items	1 Type and description stated		nr		D2 Particular specification items are those items of a fitting or ancillary nature particular to the Work Section concerned		
2 Luminaires	1 Type. size and method of fixing stated	1 Cross references to Specification	nr				
	2 Pendant, type, size and method of fixing stated	1 Drop ≤ 1.00 m					
		2 Drop > 1.00 m, drop stated					
		1 Boxes, details stated					
		2 Conduit boxes, details stated					
		3 Pattresses, details stated					
		4 Ceiling roses, details stated					
		5 Connector blocks, details stated					
		6 Flexible cords, details stated					
		7 Starters, chokes and capacitors, details stated					
		8 Shades, diffusers and reflectors, details stated					
		9 Lampholder, details stated					
		10 Conduit or chain suspension, details stated					
		11 Suspension system, details stated					
		12 Lighting columns, details					

	First column	Unit / sub	Supplementary	Measurement rules	Coverage rules
4 Luminaires and lamps provided by the Employer	1 Type, size and method of fixing stated		1 Provision of additional components and internal wiring, details stated 2 Background stated		C4 Accepting delivery, storing and handling are deemed to be included
5 Accessories	1 Type, box and method of fixing stated	nr 1 Rated capacity stated	1 Plugs to be provided with socket outlets 2 Background stated	M3 Accessories are enumerated in gangs where appropriate	C5 Plugs are deemed to include fuses
6 Disconnecting, setting aside and refixing for the convenience of other trades	1 Type of equipment and purpose of disconnection stated	item			

Y81 Testing and commissioning electrical services
Y82 Identification - electrical
Y89 Sundry common electrical items

INFORMATION PROVIDED				MEASUREMENT RULES	DEFINITION RULES	COVERAGE RULES	SUPPLEMENTARY INFORMATION
P1 Information is shown on location drawings under A Preliminaries/General conditions				M1 Work related to these Sections is classified in accordance with Sections V10 – W60 as Appendix B and given under an appropriate Work Section heading			
CLASSIFICATION TABLE							
1 Additional bonding	1 Bonding resulting from testing extraneous metal	prov sum		M2 Alternatively a Provisional Sum may be included in Section A54			
2 Marking position of holes, mortices and chases in the structure	1 Installation stated	item	1 Formed during construction, details stated				
3 Loose ancillaries	1 Keys 2 Tools 3 Spares	nr	1 Type, quality or quantity stated		1 Names of recipients		
4 Identification where not provided with equipment or control gear	1 Plates 2 Discs 3 Labels 4 Tapes and bands 5 Arrows, symbols, letters and numbers 6 Charts		1 Type, size and method of fixing stated	1 Details of engraving stated 2 Mounting of charts, details stated			
5 Testing and commissioning	1 Installation stated	item	1 Stage tests (nr) listed and purpose stated 2 Instruction of personnel in operation of completed installation	1 Attendance required 2 Instruments to be provided	C1 Provision of electricity and other supplies is deemed to be included C2 Provision of test certificates is deemed to be included	
6 Temporary operation of installations, to Employer's requirements	1 Installation and purpose of operation stated	item	1 Duration of operation period stated	M3 Provision of electricity and other supplies is covered by Provisional Sums in Section A54	1 Attendance required 2 Conditions imposed by Employer before operation allowed		

8 Operating and
maintenance manuals

2 Names of recipients
stated

item

fitted' drawings

Additional rules – work to existing buildings

Work Groups H, J, K, L and M – work to existing buildings

INFORMATION PROVIDED	MEASUREMENT RULES	DEFINITION RULES	COVERAGE RULES	SUPPLEMENTARY INFORMATION
P1 The following information is shown either on location drawings under A Preliminaries/General conditions or on further drawings which accompany the bills of quantities: (a) the scope and location of the work relative to – the existing layout indicating the existing structure – the proposed layout	M1 These rules cover each work section within the Work Groups H, J, K, L and M and apply to works to existing buildings as defined in the General Rules	D1 Materials arising from the work are the property of the Contractor unless otherwise stated	C1 Shoring and scaffolding incidental to the work and making good all work disturbed by such shoring and scaffolding is deemed to be included within each item C2 Items for work to existing buildings are deemed to include: (a) disposal of materials other than those remaining the property of the Employer or those for re-use (b) incidental work which is at the discretion of the Contractor (c) all new fixing or jointing materials required	S1 Method of operation, where by specific means S2 Setting aside and storing materials remaining the property of the Employer or those for re-use S3 Employer's restrictions on methods of disposal of materials including toxic or other special waste S4 Kind, quality and thickness of materials S5 Type of construction S6 Special trims S7 Restrictions on the method of shoring and scaffolding

CLASSIFICATION TABLE

1 Bonding/jointing new to existing	1 Dimensioned description		m²			
			m			
			nr			
2 Stripping off/removing/taking down	1 Dimensioned description	1 In preparation for replacement	m²		M3 This item is only measured separately where new work is purely extending the existing	
			m			
			nr			
	2 Spot item dimensioned description		item			C3 Spot items are deemed to include jointing /bonding new to existing

		Unit			
4 Items extra over making good disturbed work	2 Spot item dimensioned description	nr			C4 Spot items are deemed to include jointing/bonding new to existing
	1 Jointing/bonding new to existing	item			
5 Cutting	1 Raking	m			
	2 Curved				
6 Cutting holes	1 Ducts	nr	1 Girth ≤ 1.00 m 2 Girth 1.00 – 2.00 m 3 and thereafter in 1.00 m stages	1 Rectangular 2 Circular 3 Dimensioned profile description 4 Making good 5 Making good to match existing 6 Facework described	D2 Ducts include trays, trunking, gratings and the like
	2 Pipes		1 ≤ 55 mm nominal size 2 55 – 110 mm nominal size 3 > 110 mm nominal size		D3 Pipes include tubes, bars, cables, conduit and the like

R10–R13 Drainage – work to existing buildings
Y Mechanical services – work to existing buildings

CLASSIFICATION TABLE				MEASUREMENT RULES	DEFINITION RULES	COVERAGE RULES	SUPPLEMENTARY INFORMATION
1 Breaking into existing pipes 2 Breaking into existing ducts	1 Type, size and location of existing pipe or duct stated	1 Purpose of breaking in stated	item	1 Obtaining approval for isolation where necessary 2 Isolating existing pipe or duct 3 Isolating and draining down existing pipe 4 Preparing ends of existing for new work 5 Limitations to shut down period			
3 Jointing new pipes to existing 4 Jointing new ducts to existing	1 Type, size of both pipes or ducts and method of jointing stated		nr	1 Preparing ends of existing pipes and ducts where not taken with 1 – 2.1.1.4		C1 Providing everything necessary for jointing is deemed to be included	
5 Stripping out part installations 6 Stripping out whole installations	1 Dimensioned description detailing extent and location 2 Spot item dimensioned description		nr item	1 Obtaining approval for isolation where necessary 2 Isolating part or whole to be removed 3 Isolating and draining down part or whole to be rescued 4 Making safe 5 Limitations to shut down period			
7 Provision of temporary services, bypasses and the like	1 Dimensioned description		nr	1 Fabrication prior to installation		C2 Provision of temporary services, bypasses and the like is deemed to include removing and making good after	
				M1 Alternatively this work may be measured in accordance with the Rules for new work and grouped under an appropriate heading			
8 Stripping off insulation to part of services installations 9 Stripping off insulation to whole services installations	1 Dimensioned description detailing extent and location 2 Spot item dimensioned description	1 Type of insulation to be removed	nr item	1 Safety measures to be applied 2 Disposal requirements			

mechanical installations

purpose stated

3 Insurance Company tests, if any, details stated

4 Instruction of personnel in operation of completed installation

3 Special insurance requirements of Employer stated

included

C4 Provision of test certificates is deemed to be included

Y Electrical services - work to existing buildings

CLASSIFICATION TABLE				MEASUREMENT RULES	DEFINITION RULES	COVERAGE RULES	SUPPLEMENTARY INFORMATION
1 Cables drawn into existing conduits or ducts or laid or drawn in existing trunking 2 Cables laid or drawn into existing trunking and laced into circuit groups	1 Type, size, number of cores, armouring and sheathing stated	1 Type and size of existing conduit or duct stated 2 Type and size of existing trunking stated	m	M1 Except for final circuits cables in conduits or trunking and cables fixed to trays are measured as the net length of the conduit, trunking or tray. Other cables are measured as fixed without allowance for sag M2 The following allowances shall be made: (a) 0.30 m on each cable entering fittings, luminaires or accessories (b) 0.60 m on each cable entering equipment or control gear	D1 Cables are defined as being laced into circuit groups only where this is specified	C1 Cables and tapes are deemed to include: (a) wall, floor and ceiling plates (b) cable sleeves C2 Cables laid or drawn into existing conduits, existing ducts or existing trunking is deemed to include removing and replacing existing covers, existing inspection lids and the like	S1 Details of colour coding or other markings of cables for phase identification
3 Breaking into existing cables 4 Breaking into existing equipment and control gear	1 Type, size and location of existing cable, equipment or control gear stated	1 Purpose of breaking in stated, details of associated conduit, trunking or tray given	nr				
		1 Obtaining approval to isolation where necessary 2 Isolating existing cable, equipment or control gear 3 Preparing existing for jointing of new work					
5 Jointing new cables to existing 6 Jointing new equipment and control gear to existing 7 Jointing new conduits, trunking and trays to existing	1 Type, size of both new and existing work and method of jointing stated	1 Preparing existing for jointing to new where not taken with 3–4.1.1.3 2 Joint boxes, type stated 3 Sealing boxes, type stated 4 Shrouds, type stated 5 Boxes, type stated 6 Special boxes, type stated 7 Other components, type stated	nr			C3 Providing everything necessary for jointing is deemed included	
8 Stripping out part installations 9 Stripping out whole installations	1 Dimensioned description detailing extent and location 2 Spot item dimensioned description	1 Obtaining approval for isolation where necessary 2 Isolating whole or part to be removed 3 Making safe 4 Limitations to shut down	nr item				

			item		new work and grouped under an appropriate heading	making good after
11 Testing and commissioning existing electrical installations	1 Part installation stated 2 Whole installation stated			1 Stage tests (nr) listed and purpose stated 2 Instruction of personnel in operation of completed installation	1 Attendance required 2 Instruments to be provided 3 Special insurance requirements of Employer stated	C5 Provision of electricity and other supplies is deemed to be included C6 Provision of test certificates is deemed to be included

Appendix A

Fixtures, furnishings, equipment, fittings and appliances as referred to in the rules for Work Sections N10, N11, N12, N13, N15, N16, N20-N23, P21 and Q50

N10 General fixtures/furnishings/equipment

Furnishings, fittings and equipment, fixed to the building fabric or provided loose within the building, and 'general' in the sense that they may be found in a wide variety of buildings. Culinary and sanitary furnishings, fittings and equipment are excluded, together with items which would normally be included in building services sub-contracts. Minor items of special purpose equipment may be included here rather than in sections N20–N23 'Special purpose fixtures/furnishings/equipment'.

Included

Counters, desks, benches, worktops
Small mirrors in toilets, dressing rooms
Curtain track and rails
Curtains, loose wall hangings, fabrics, blinds
Fireplaces, surrounds and hearths
Telephone booths and enclosures
Storage racks, shelves, shelving support systems
Door mats, matwells
Wall hangings, loose carpets
Lockers, hat and coat rails
General purpose chairs and tables
Fitted seating, upholstery
Beds, divans
Wardrobes, dressers, cupboards, cabinets, drawers
Objets d'art and other ornamental features, mirrors
Vending machines
Fire extinguishers
Bins
Safes
Vacuum cleaners, cleaning equipment

N11 Domestic kitchen fittings

Domestic kitchen equipment of all kinds including units, worktops, cupboards, sinks, cookers, grills, refrigerators, etc.

Included

Kitchen units, including base units, drawer units, worktops, hanging cupboards
Ovens, cookers, hobs, grills
Sinks, taps, waste fittings, waste disposal units where supplied as part of the kitchen fitting installation.
Refrigerators, freezers
Dishwashers
Clothes washing machines, clothes dryers, ironing cabinets
Waste bins, towel rails, storage racks and other accessories
Kitchen equipment suites comprising any combination of the foregoing
Fixing

N12 Catering Equipment

Culinary equipment designed for use in provision of food and drink on a communal or commercial scale.

Included

Food storage equipment other than cold rooms
Food preparation and cooking equipment
Food transporting and serving equipment
Serving counters and tray rails
Sinks where supplied as part of the catering equipment installation
Dishwashing and waste disposal equipment
Fixing

N20 – N23 Special purpose fixtures/furnishings/equipment

Furnishings, fittings and equipment, fixed to the building fabric or provided loose within the building, and 'special' in the sense that they are designed for the particular purpose(s) of the building and are likely to be obtained from a specialist supplier or contractor. The title(s) of the section(s) should indicate the nature of the special purpose equipment, e.g. 'Special purpose hospital fixtures/furnishings/equipment'. Four work section numbers have been allocated to provide for projects with several types of special purpose fixtures, furnishings and equipment.

General purpose, culinary and sanitary fixtures, fittings and equipment are excluded, together with items which would normally be included in building services sub-contracts. Minor items of special purpose equipment may be included in section N10 'General fixtures/furnishings/equipment' rather than here.

Included

Fixtures, fittings and equipment for special purposes, including:
Rail, road, water and air transport buildings, terminals
Communications, power supply, mineral supply, water supply buildings
Agricultural, fishing and forestry buildings
Factories/industrial buildings for food, drink, chemicals, engineering, textiles, clay, cement, timber, construction, etc.
Administrative, office and commercial buildings
Shops, showrooms, stores, shopping centres, warehouses
Defence, police, prison and fire service buildings
Hospital, medical, welfare and animal welfare buildings
Restaurants, snack bars, public houses
Entertainment buildings, community centres, clubs
Sports buildings, swimming pools, marinas, stadia
Religious buildings, funerary buildings
Educational buildings including scientific research facilities
Libraries, record offices, museums, galleries, zoos
Special residential buildings, hotels, old peoples' homes

N15 Signs/notices

Directories, notice boards, letters, signs, plaques, symbols and emblems of all kinds for identification and directional purposes.

Included

Signwriting
Lettering, emblems and other identification/directional symbols carved onto stone
Door or floor numbering or lettering
Name plates, plaques and identification symbols of all materials
Directional signboards and notice boards of all kinds and materials
Shop front lettering, emblems and symbols of all kinds and materials
Illuminated signs, lettering, emblems and symbols such as "Exit" signs, "Gentlemen", etc. where the illuminated fitting is simply connected to an adjacent electrical outlet

N16 Bird/Vermin control

Installations to repel, trap or otherwise control birds or vermin which may be a nuisance or danger to health.

Included

Wires, nets, traps
Repellent coatings
Electronic/sonic systems

N13 Sanitary appliances/fittings

Appliances for health, hygiene and personal washing, together with their accessories, but excluding sinks for domestic kitchens.

Included

WC pans and cisterns, WC suites
Slop hoppers
Urinals and cisterns
Sinks, including kitchen sinks not supplied as part of the kitchen fitting installation, and catering sinks not supplied as part of the catering equipment installation
Wash basins
Hand rinse basins
Wash fountains
Bidets
Baths
Bath panels and trim
Jacuzzis
Shower cubicles, shower trays
Bath/shower curtain rails, screens, etc.
Instantaneous shower heaters
Drinking fountains
Vanity units
Grab/support rails
Taps and waste fittings to the appliances
Float operated valves
Bath panels and trim
Hand dryers
Towel rails and holders not connected to a heating or hot water supply installation
Paper towel dispensers
Toilet paper holders
Waste bins
Soap dispensers and holders
Sanitary incinerators
Sanitary macerators
Saunas, sauna equipment

P21 Door/Window Ironmongery

Components and items of metal, plastics and other materials, used to hang, fasten, close and/or open, secure, seal and furnish doors and windows, and supplied separately therefrom, whether fixed on or off site.

Included

Sliding and up and over door tracks or overhead rails; hangers, guides and fittings

Sash balances

Butts, hinges, pivots and other opening/closing devices

Spring butts, door springs, door closers and other self closing devices

Locks, latches, catches, cylinder locks, nightlatches and other locking devices

Bolts, panic bolts, espagnolette bolts, security bolts, casement and sash fasteners and other securing devices

Door handles, escutcheons, casement stays, sash pulls, letter plates, kicking plates, push plates, pull handles, trickle ventilators and other door and window furniture

Door stops, retaining devices, draughtproofing strips and sections

Nameplates, numbers, knockers, bell pushes, door viewers

Mechanical and/or automatic operating or opening equipment where not supplied with the component or installed as part of an access control installation

Q50 Site/Street furniture/equipment

General purpose furniture and equipment designed for use externally, but excluding items provided by a statutory undertaker, authority or services sub-contractor

Included

Gates and lifting barriers, where not part of fencing (Q40) or barriers/guardrails (Q41)

Bollards (including removable and collapsible)

Seats, benches, tables

Litter bins, grit bins, dustbins

Poster display units or hoardings

Cycle stands other than precast concrete slabs (see section Q25)

Flagpoles

Minor footbridges

Clothes drying fittings

Sculptures and other ornamental features

Sports and playground equipment

Other special purpose equipment occurring externally

Excavation, concrete backfilling for foundations

Appendix B

Classification of mechanical and electrical services as referred to in the rules for Work Group Y

R Disposal systems

R14 Laboratory/Industrial waste drainage
R20 Sewage pumping
R21 Sewage treatment/sterilisation
R30 Centralised vacuum cleaning
R31 Refuse chutes
R32 Compactors/Macerators
R33 Incineration plant

S Piped supply systems

S10 Cold water
S11 Hot water
S12 Hot and cold water (self-contained specification)
S13 Pressurised water
S14 Irrigation
S15 Fountains/Water features
S20 Treated/Deionised/Distilled water
S21 Swimming pool water treatment
S30 Compressed air
S31 Instrument air
S32 Natural gas
S33 Liquified petroleum gas
S34 Medical/Laboratory gas
S40 Petrol/Diesel storage/distribution
S41 Fuel oil storage/distribution
S50 Vacuum
S51 Steam
S60 Fire hose reels
S61 Dry risers
S62 Wet risers
S63 Sprinklers
S64 Deluge
S65 Fire hydrants
S70 Gas fire fighting
S71 Foam fire fighting

T Mechanical heating/Cooling/Refrigeration systems

T10 Gas/Oil fired boilers
T11 Coal fired boilers
T12 Electrode/Direct electric boilers
T13 Packaged steam generators
T14 Heat pumps
T15 Solar collectors
T16 Alternative fuel boilers
T20 Primary heat distribution
T30 Medium temperature hot water heating
T31 Low temperature hot water heating
T32 Low temperature hot water heating (self-contained specification)
T33 Steam heating
T40 Warm air heating
T41 Warm air heating (self-contained specification)
T42 Local heating units
T50 Heat recovery
T60 Central refrigeration plant
T61 Chilled water
T70 Local cooling units
T71 Cold rooms
T72 Ice pads

U Ventilation/Air conditioning systems

U10 General ventilation
U11 Toilet ventilation
U12 Kitchen ventilation
U13 Car parking ventilation
U14 Smoke extract/ Smoke control
U15 Safety cabinet/Fume cupboard extract
U16 Fume extract
U17 Anaesthetic gas extract
U20 Dust collection
U30 Low velocity air conditioning
U31 VAV air conditioning
U32 Dual-duct air conditioning
U33 Multi-zone air conditioning
U40 Induction air conditioning
U41 Fan-coil air conditioning
U42 Terminal re-heat air conditioning
U43 Terminal heat pump air conditioning
U50 Hybrid system air conditioning
U60 Air conditioning units
U70 Air curtains

V Electrical supply/power/ lighting systems

V10 Electricity generation plant
V11 HV supply/distribution/public utility supply
V12 LV supply/public utility supply
V20 LV distribution
V21 General lighting
V22 General LV power
V30 Extra low voltage supply
V31 DC supply
V32 Uninterruptable power supply
V40 Emergency lighting
V41 Street/Area/Flood lighting
V42 Studio/Auditorium/Arena lighting
V50 Electric underfloor/ceiling heating
V51 Local electric heating units
V90 Electrical installation (self-contained specification)

W Communications/Security/ Control systems

W10 Telecommunications
W11 Paging/Emergency call
W12 Public address/Conference audio facilities
W20 Radio/TV/CCTV
W21 Projection
W22 Information/Advertising display
W23 Clocks
W30 Data transmission
W40 Access control
W41 Security detection and alarm
W50 Fire detection and alarm
W51 Earthing and bonding
W52 Lightning protection
W53 Electromagnetic screening
W54 Liquid detection alarm
W60 Central control/Building management

Alphabetical Index

188